New Nelson Handwriting

Teacher's Manual

Peter Smith and A. Inglis

Nelson

Thomas Nelson and Sons Ltd
Nelson House Mayfield Road
Walton-on-Thames Surrey KT12 5PL

51 York Place Edinburgh EH1 3JD UK

Thomas Nelson (Hong Kong) Ltd
Toppan Building 10/F
22A Westlands Road
Quarry Bay Hong Kong

Distributed in Australia by

Thomas Nelson Australia
480 La Trobe Street
Melbourne Victoria 3000
and in Sydney, Brisbane, Adelaide and Perth

First edition published by Thomas Nelson & Sons Ltd 1961
Second edition published by Thomas Nelson & Sons Ltd 1984
Third edition published by Thomas Nelson & Sons Ltd 1989

ISBN 0-17-424138-0
NPN 987654321

Printed in Great Britain by Bell and Bain Ltd., Glasgow

Contents

Part 2 Using the Pupils' Books and the Copymasters 61

A ready reference guide to the main features of the scheme

1. How *New Nelson Handwriting* is organised

Pupils' Book A
- Pencil play and pattern practice
- Introduction of lower-case letters, words and numerals

handwriting

Pupils' Book B
- Revision of patterns and lower-case Infant Writing
- Introduction of capitals
- A spelling resource for creative writing

Handwriting

Pupils' Book 1
- Revision of print script and joining patterns
- Logical introduction and practice of all joins for joined writing

Handwriting

Pupils' Book 2
- Revision of joins
- Developing quality and fluency in joined writing
- Developing good spelling strategies

Handwriting

Pupils' Book 3
- Revision of joins
- Developing sloping writing
- Introduction of ink writing
- Good spelling strategies

Handwriting

Handwriting

Pupils' Book 4
- Revision of joins
- Quality and fluency in ink writing
- Shaded writing
- Developing an individual style

Handwriting

Handwriting

Infant Copymasters
- Additional practice for pencil exercises, Infant Writing, words and exercises

Infant Big Book
- Help with letter formation and co-ordination skills, working on a large scale with groups

Early Practice Books (X3)
- Writing patterns
- Letters and numerals
- Capital letters and how to use them

Junior Copymasters
- Additional practice in learning joins and models for sustained writing practice

Teacher's Manual
- A complete guide to the theory and practice of teaching handwriting
- Page by page guide to teaching the Pupils' Books

2. The Infant Writing alphabet and the numerals taught in Pupils' Books A and B

a b c d e f g h i j k l m

n o p q r s t u v w x y z

A B C D E F G H I J

K L M N O P Q R S

T U V W X Y Z

0 1 2 3 4 5 6 7 8 9

3. The basic alphabet used in Nelson joined writing

a b c d e f g h i j k

l m n o p q r s t u v

w x y z

4. The join sets used in Nelson joined writing

Set 1

The set of lower-case letters which have hooks at the bottom of the 'x' height:

a c d e h i k l m n t u

Set 2

The set of lower-case letters which are written commencing at the top of the 'x' height:

a c d e g i j m n o p q

r s u v w x y

Set 3

The set of lower-case letters which are written commencing at the top of the ascender:

b f h k l t

Set 4

The set of lower-case letters which are concluded at the top of the 'x' height:

f o r v w

Set 5

The set of lower-case letters *after* which no join is ever made:

b g j p q s x y z

No join is ever made *to z* either.

5. The rules for joining

The basic join

The join from any member of Set 1 to any member of Set 2:

The second join

The join from any member of Set 1 to any member of Set 3:

The third join

The join from any member of Set 4 to any member of Set 2:

The fourth join

The join from any member of Set 4 to any member of Set 3:

The break letters

No join is ever made *after* the break letters. No join is ever made *to z* either.

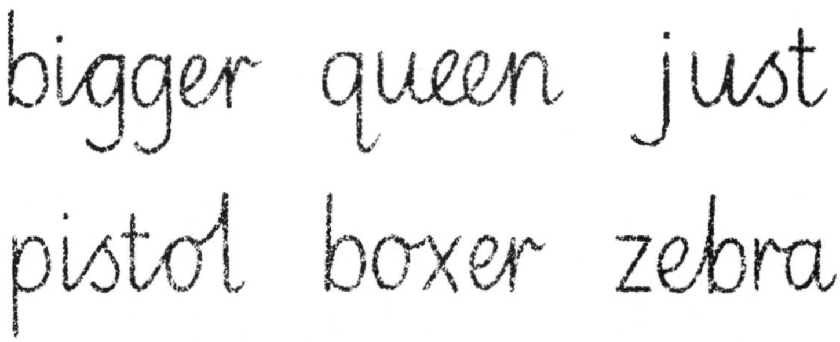

6. The size of writing in each book

Infant	Junior
Pupils' Book A little	Pupils' Book 1 little
	Pupils' Book 2 little
Pupils' Book B little	Pupils' Book 3 little
	Pupils' Book 4 little

Part 1

Basic Principles

1 Introduction

Aim of the scheme

The aim of this scheme is for all children to acquire, in the words of the Bullock Report, 'a running hand which is simultaneously legible, fast-flowing and individual', so that children can write clearly, fluently and quickly and thus cope with the everyday writing demands of life and school. At the same time it aims to teach good writing habits and pleasant letter forms as well as to encourage pride in calligraphy and the aesthetic qualities of presentation when appropriate.

Organisation

The core scheme consists of six Pupils' Books backed by this Teacher's Manual. There are also two books of copymasters to provide additional practice at the Infant and Junior levels respectively. Recent, supplementary publications include the Infant Big Book and three Early Practice Books, all of which support and extend the Infant levels. An outline chart explaining the scheme's structure will be found on page 1 in the Ready Reference section of this manual and at the front of each Pupils' Book.

Pupils' Books A and B teach the Infant Writing. Pupils' Books 1–4 provide a course in joined writing from the introduction of the Nelson joined style to the development of an individual style. The second edition of *Nelson Handwriting* was reorganised so that all joins are taught in a concentrated fashion in Pupils' Book 1. Then, as progress is made through the remaining books, ample revision and practice in joining is provided. In addition there are exercises to promote fluency and speed and children are encouraged to assess their own progress and to check over their written work for mistakes. In Pupils' Book 3 children are encouraged to slope their writing to the right and writing with pen and ink is introduced. Finally, in Pupils' Book 4, individuality of style is actively encouraged and broad nib writing is introduced as one possible development from the basic Nelson style.

It is impossible to be prescriptive about the ages at which children should use each of the books in the series. Since at all stages in their development, children are likely to vary considerably in the level of their skills and abilities, groups of children within any class, but particularly in the Infant classes, may need to work with different books in the scheme. However, provided that teachers are prepared to be flexible in meeting the needs of individual children, the following guidelines should prove helpful:

Pupils' Book	Stage	Age
A	Reception/Middle Infant	4½–6
B	Middle/Top Infant	5½–7
1	First Year Junior	7–8
2	Second Year Junior	8–9
3	Third Year Junior	9–10
4	Fourth Year Junior	10–11

Changes from the first edition

Although the scheme has been substantially revised, it is still firmly based on the calligraphic style and structure of the original *Nelson Handwriting* published in 1961. Revisions in 1984 and 1989 have taken account of current thinking about handwriting, changes in teaching approach and a detailed questionnaire to many schools using *Nelson Handwriting*.

The main focus of the 1984 revision was directed towards improvement in fluency and rhythm of the style by increasing the number of natural joins. Other major changes include improved continuity from the Infant Writing to joined writing, an accelerated pace for introducing the rules for joining and a greater emphasis on the swings pattern because of its significance as the basic join. The 1989 edition takes particular account of handwriting in the context of writing generally.

In detail the changes are as follows:

1. Changes to some Infant Writing letter shapes

	Original edition	1984 edition
Lower case letters		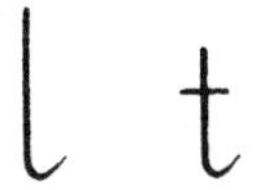
Capital letters		
Numerals	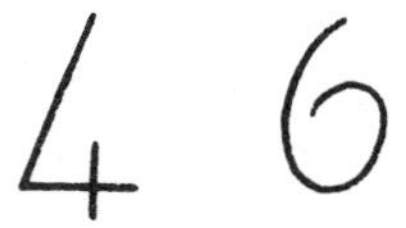	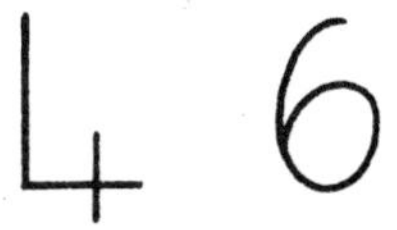

2. Earlier and more logical introduction of joins allowing more joins to take place

All joins are now taught in a concentrated fashion in Pupils' Book 1 rather than being spread over three books. The rules for joining have been simplified into a logical system with clear rules, which are discussed on page 44 of this manual.

Some letters alter their shape at times in the joined style to allow more joins to take place:

	Original edition	**1984 edition**
Letter shape	e	e e
Example	re	re
Letter shape	s	s s s
Example	ds rs	ds rs

The following letters which were never joined in the first edition are now joined:

a c d e h i k l m n t u are now joined to b f h k l t and a c d g o q
f o r v w are now joined to b e f h k l s t

3. A new emphasis on the link between handwriting and spelling

An increasing number of teachers are adopting new strategies with regard to spelling because of a growing dissatisfaction with some former practices. For example, the practice of artificially limiting children's written vocabulary by providing a pre-determined group of words often led to banal, stilted writing. Another once common practice, the provision of individual alphabetic word books with which children queued for teachers to provide spellings, interfered with their flow of language and resulted in time-wasting.

The current trend in spelling in the early years is towards 'invented spelling', which requires children to try a spelling without worrying about whether it is correct. There are several advantages to this approach: children are encouraged to make their own sense of the sound/symbol relationships; their fluency is not interrupted by queueing to see the teacher; and errors which arise provide useful diagnostic tools for teachers.

Of course, it can still be useful to draw attention to the spelling of specialist words relating to a common theme, but even here the expectations would be different. Children would no longer be expected to learn spellings by rote nor to copy them mindlessly. Rather, they would be involved in discussion of the letter strings employed and, instead of blind copying, they would be encouraged to use the routine discussed on page 114 of this manual: look, cover, write and check.

Similarly, the practice of checking spellings against dictionaries (and other sources such as captions in the classroom) is recommended.

It must be remembered that the introduction of an innovative approach, like invented spelling, does necessitate explanation to parents, including the need to demonstrate clearly that the school does have a policy to ensure that pupils eventually master the intricacies of conventional spelling. *New Nelson Handwriting* was deliberately designed to incorporate just such a programme.

The research of Margaret Peters into the natural link between handwriting and spelling is acknowledged, and an attempt has been made to contribute to the development of good spelling. The word lists in Pupils' Book B have been designed as a spelling resource for free writing by six and seven year-olds. Books 2 and 3 feature special practice pages chosen to consolidate pupils' mastery of common spelling rules and to develop both a visual and motor memory of the spelling patterns.

4. Modernisation of the models for practice

More contemporary and appropriate practice material now appears in the Pupils' Books. This includes not only modern poems and prose extracts but functional materials, such as lists, recipes and maths problems, to reflect a wider range of classroom activities including natural history and science.

5. Modernisation of format

The format of the books has been modernised and simplified to make them easier to use.

The amount of instruction printed in the Pupils' Books has been kept to a minimum. Much of the advice previously printed in the Pupils' Books has been included in the second part of this manual.

6. Reduction of the two teacher's manuals into one

The two teacher's manuals that accompanied the original edition have been replaced by a single volume so that teachers working at any stage in the Primary School may be aware of what has gone before and what will follow. Every attempt has been made to write the necessary notes of guidance as succinctly as possible so that busy teachers can find and use the information quickly and easily.

7. Developments since 1984

Since the 1984 edition of the Teacher's Manual to accompany *New Nelson Handwriting* was prepared, there has been greatly increased awareness of the writing process and the ways in which children progress in their understanding of, and competence in, the complex skills involved.

The work undertaken through the *National Writing Project*, and through many publications and research reports from all over the world, has focused on fundamental principles of communication and purpose. Such terms as 'emergent writing', 'developmental writing', 'audience', 'planning', 'drafting', 'revising', 'editing' and 'publishing' are now commonplace among teachers discussing children's writing. At the same time, attitudes to the secretarial skills of writing are also becoming more enlightened and terms such as 'dictated writing', 'collaborative writing', 'shared writing' and 'invented spelling' all indicate new thinking.

However, in order for there to be balance in the provision to meet children's real needs, schools also need well thought out policies for handwriting and spelling. These are essential if children's first attempts at writing are not to be inhibited by undue emphasis on precision in basic skills and yet the children are eventually to become fluent, legible writers and accurate, conventional spellers. It was, indeed, just this balance between motivation and purpose on the one hand and the desire to achieve competence in the traditional secretarial skills on the other hand, that led to the original revision of *Nelson Handwriting*.

In the earliest stages, guidance is given to teachers to assist them in sensitive intervention in ways which reflect the stages of development of children. The models and exercises provided then continue to support busy teachers and to encourage children as they grow towards mastery and confidence in their ability to write legibly and spell accurately, as well as continuing to write in a lively manner for a variety of purposes.

The importance of individuality

The models in the Pupils' Books are intended to guide teachers in deciding on an appropriate sequence of learning steps as well as providing pupils with accurate and attractive examples as a basis for practice. It is not intended that pupils at any stage in learning to write should be required or expected to make exact reproductions of the letter forms presented as models in the Pupils' Books. Indeed, it is far more important that children learn to form letters and effect joins correctly than it is for them to produce a perfect copy of the model, the process being more important than the product at this stage. Moreover, in due course it is likely that many children will develop individual variations on the basic Nelson style. These variations will give their writing character and, provided they do not detract from the legibility of their writing, are to be encouraged. In addition, the fluency and rhythm of the children's hand movements should lend their writing a pleasing grace. These qualities are naturally lacking in the more formal and stereotyped models provided in the Pupils' Books.

Letter forms and style

The letter forms introduced in the first book are very similar to the print used in most recent reading schemes so that both aspects of literacy, reading and writing, consolidate each other. The shapes, particularly the oval bodies of *a*, *b*, *c*, *d*, *g*, *o*, *p* and *q*, were chosen because oval forms are more easily produced than round forms, and the making of letters in one continuous movement is more readily achieved. These simple lower-case letter forms learned in the early years are then developed gradually, with only minor modifications, throughout the scheme. Even at the stage of joining, there are no major alterations to the letter shapes so that those children who may be still learning to read are not confused by a sudden lack of correspondence between the letter forms they see in print and those they are expected to write. The same is true of capital letters which are kept plain and simple. They remain unchanged throughout the scheme and are never joined to lower-case letters.

Size of writing

The size of writing appropriate for a particular stage in a child's development depends on the individual's neuromuscular development and co-ordination, the writing instrument being used and the expectation implied by the size of model provided. The policy adopted in this scheme involves a gradual reduction of writing size as the pupils develop, and care has been taken to ensure that the size of models in each of the Pupils' Books is appropriate for the children who will use it. However, it is important to remember that not all children in a group can be reasonably expected to write exactly the same size. The writing sizes for each book can be found in the Ready Reference section on page 5.

Word processors and typewriters

A teacher's manual on handwriting would be incomplete without reference to the exciting possibilities of word processing. Throughout the 1980s, there has been a steady increase in the availability of computers with word processing facilities in primary and middle schools. Alongside this improved resourcing, which includes some innovative software, has come increased knowledge and confidence in the ability to use this new technology. Teachers and pupils are mastering the techniques involved and enjoying the resulting opportunities for easy revision, efficient editing and instant ability to produce multiple copies.

Children have clearly demonstrated the ease with which they acquire keyboard skills and there is every reason to expect that future generations will make good use of word processors. It also seems likely that more use will be made of typewriters, including those with 'jumbo' type which can be particularly useful for very young or visually impaired children. Indeed, the value of typewriters for use by children with physical handicaps is already widely recognised.

However, it must be emphasised that to appreciate the role of typewriters and word processors is not to denigrate the importance of the traditional skill of handwriting. Every child will still need help to achieve maximum progress towards the attainment of an efficient personal handwriting style.

2 Teaching method

The role of the teacher

There is no universally agreed formula for success in teaching handwriting. However, the teacher's role in demonstrating the formation of letters and patterns and also in supervising children's practice cannot be over-emphasised. Since the teaching of handwriting is generally accepted to be largely a matter of teaching movements, the importance of competent demonstration is obvious. It therefore follows that teachers will want to develop their own confidence in producing the necessary movements speedily and rhythmically both on paper and on blackboards or when using alternative teaching aids. (There are implications here for those responsible for the initial training of teachers as well as for in-service courses.) Many experienced teachers have devised their own techniques for motivating and instructing their pupils and the bibliography lists several books, including the author's publication, *Developing Handwriting*, which contain useful hints.

While the children practise the models in the Pupils' Books the teacher should supervise and observe them carefully. With experience, teachers learn to detect *significant* faults and are able to help individuals to correct them before they become habits. Faults which become ingrained in the early stages are very difficult to eradicate later. However, teachers will need to be flexible in their appraisals and to appreciate that some children may write well without necessarily adhering totally to recommendations. Problems to watch for are those bad habits which may handicap the writer's proper development at any stage. Some faults of posture or pencil grip, for instance, do not prevent some degree of success in the early stages when pencil is the main writing tool but may cause serious problems when the transition to pen is made. Points to watch for are more fully discussed in Chapter 11: Significant faults.

Terms to use

To teach handwriting effectively it is often helpful to use specific technical terms to describe the various hand movements and letter features. *New Nelson Handwriting* consciously employs a simple technical vocabulary in Pupils' Books 1–4. Teachers will find it helpful to explain clearly these terms to pupils as they arise.

The following terms are introduced in the Pupils' Books:

Book 1	Book 2	Book 4
p. 2 Infant Writing	p. 1 spiral	p. 1 clockwise
p. 3 joined	p. 2 down-stroke	anticlockwise
p. 4 lower-case		p. 3 parallel
p. 5 up-stroke		p. 19 shaded writing
p. 6 capitals		straight-edged pen
ascenders		vertical
descenders		p. 20 uphill
ordinary		downhill
p. 7 upswing		running
p. 13 diagonally		p. 26 flourish
p. 19 horizontal		

While a full definition of these and other terms will be found in the glossary at the back of this manual, it seems worthwhile to draw particular attention to one important aspect of the terminology used here. Since letters with ascenders are just as tall as capital letters, it seems misleading to refer to letters which are not capitals as *small letters*. For this reason the printing term *lower-case* has been used to denote such letters. In addition, to help children differentiate between the three types of lower-case letter, letters without ascenders or descenders have been called *ordinary letters*.

In Pupils' Books A and B there are no written instructions so teachers are free to decide whether to introduce this terminology where appropriate, or not. Many Infant teachers will prefer to use more descriptive and imaginative language to describe hand movements and letter shapes. Examples of 'fun' terminology are too numerous to document fully in this manual but examples from two mnemonical systems to help children remember letter shapes may be included here:

1) From Ruth Fagg's *Everyday Writing*.

Letter *s* is a swan who holds her head high.

2) From Lyn Wendon's *Pictograms*.

DIPPY DUCK

Stroke Dippy's back.
Go **round** his tum.

Go **up** his neck.
Then **down** you come!

Actual letter size: 10 cm, with plain letter on reverse side of each card, for convenient finger tracing. Capital and small letter on alphabet friezes the same size (10 cm).

In *Pictograms* Lyn Wendon has evolved a comprehensive system of associations for all the letters of the alphabet.

Whatever terminology is used, children will need to understand a number of important concepts as they learn the letter shapes in Pupils' Books A and B. The main concepts are as follows:

clockwise
anticlockwise
vertical
up
down
horizontal (across)
diagonal
round (circular)
straight

ascender
descender
lower-case
capital letter
left to right
curved
height (of letters)
width (of letters)
circle
oval

Some suggestions as to where technical teminology might be introduced in Pupils' Books A and B will be found in the relevant page by page guide in Part 2 of this manual.

Recommended sizes of teaching groups

The decision as to whether to teach handwriting to individuals, groups or the whole class is, to some extent, a matter of personal preference. However, bearing in mind the need for sensible economy in time and effort, many teachers may find the following suggestions acceptable.

1. At the beginning stage (Pupils' Book A) it is probably helpful to teach children in groups according to their stages of development and degree of readiness although as much individual help as possible should be given during practice sessions.

2. Later in the Infant stage (Pupils' Book B) it should be possible to give revision lessons and further instruction to whole classes since, although children's skill levels will vary still, by this stage they should all understand the fundamental concepts of written language.

3. Similarly, at the stage of introducing joined writing (Pupils' Book 1) it is economical to work with whole classes with extra group or individual help as appropriate.

Allocating time

Throughout the primary school regular lessons for teaching and revising are necessary. Opinion differs as to whether a few minutes daily or longer periods, perhaps twice a week, are more effective. There are, however, two specific points in the handwriting programme where a greater allocation of time is advisable:

1. At the very beginning of formal instruction (Pupils' Book A)

Children need to learn the correct way to form all of the letters as quickly as possible otherwise they may try to write letters they have not been taught and so acquire unfortunate writing habits.

2. When joined writing is taught (Pupils' Book 1)

The programme of instruction in the techniques involved in joined writing may well commence when children are seven or eight years old. As it is hoped that the children will have been motivated to want to change to joined writing, it seems sensible to provide a 'crash course' with several lessons a week to establish correct procedures.

3 Writing materials

Writing implements

The Infant stage

Pupils' Book A

At the pre-writing and beginning stages, children enjoy and benefit from making bold left-to-right patterns and free-flowing movements, using a variety of writing implements including:

finger paints	felt-tipped pens
brushes	coloured pencils
chalks	thick lead pencils
thick crayons	standard lead pencils

Then, as children begin to understand and experiment with the purposes of writing, they try to communicate with a variety of writing instruments. Increasingly, they tend to prefer pencil. At this stage, some children find a pencil with a thick stem and soft black lead most appropriate. For such children, ordinary slim pencils seem to result in the adoption of too tight a grip as they try to control them. A tight grip may, in turn, lead to tension and to a pencil held closer to the point than is desirable. On the other hand, however, there seem to be children who are perfectly at ease with a standard pencil from the very beginning.

Accordingly, it is recommended that both kinds of pencil are available in the writing areas, as well as other writing implements and a variety of kinds of paper. Experience indicates that most children make an appropriate choice when left to themselves. However, observant teachers will be ready to intervene with alternative suggestions, if necessary.

Pupils' Book B

At a later stage, when children have developed a degree of mastery over their writing instruments and their fine motor skills have improved. They will make use of standard pencils and conventional coloured pencils.

Teachers will appreciate that a danger arising from writing with pencil is that it is possible to write with a pencil no matter how it is held. It is, therefore, incumbent on teachers to ensure that children form a habit of holding their pencils in the recommended fashion so that they will also achieve success when their grip is transferred to other instruments (see pp. 27–29). Even so, children will need guidance in handling different writing tools and encouragement to experiment and to familiarise themselves with the necessary variations in grip and pressure.

The Junior stage

As children enter the Junior classes they are likely to come into contact with a wide range of writing tools including fountain pens, ballpoints, roller ball pens, nylon tips and fibre tips. There are, of course, many points of view about the use of pens and other writing tools but there is an increasing tendency to adopt a liberal and common-sense attitude to them. The following recommendations may be helpful:

Pupils' Books 1–2

At the stage of development when children are using these books the main writing tool should be the standard pencil, although some children may also bring ballpoint or other mono-line instruments to school and will expect to be allowed to use them for some of their work.

Pupils' Book 3

At about this level it is helpful to encourage children to provide themselves with a suitable fountain pen with an appropriate nib for use in some of their written work, such as for displays or special presentations. A smooth, firm, rounded nib is best for beginners. On no account should a finely pointed, flexible nib be used. Left-handers may benefit from using a nib that is specially angled.

Pupils' Book 4

Part of Book 4 is devoted to encouraging children to take an interest in calligraphy, and for some children it will be appropriate to introduce the broad nibbed pen and the technique of shaded writing.

Paper

Teachers tend to have personal preferences about the types of paper and books for use when practising handwriting. However, it will be useful to discuss some of the many alternatives and to suggest a sequence that has proved successful.

Pupils' Book A

In the very early stages small children are encouraged to make easy free-flowing movements and to produce large patterns, letters and words. They use thick writing instruments and tend to work quickly. Indeed, fluency is lost when hand-movements are slow and painstaking. Therefore, it seems sensible to use large sheets of cheap paper such as blank newsprint or thin sugar paper. If a book is preferred then the familiar drawing book containing about 20 sheets of cheap paper approximately 30 × 30cm is suitable.

Pupils' Book B, 1–4

As children's skill increases, the size of their writing can be expected to decrease and standard exercise books are then suitable for formal handwriting practice. Even older pupils who have mastered the Nelson handwriting style continue to need a special book for the occasional revision exercise. At this stage of development the provision of a second book to serve as a personal anthology can prove highly motivating. These books should be gradually compiled over the last two or three years, and the children should think of them as collections of beautiful extracts beautifully written.

Blank or ruled paper

This is another controversial issue and one on which teachers tend to hold quite strong views. What seems to be the majority viewpoint and is certainly the author's recommendation follows.

In the early stages plain paper should be used for handwriting practice as the provision of lines would introduce unnecessary difficulties. The space between the lines inevitably predetermines the size of the writing, thus compelling an unnatural conformity.

Most children respond to advice and instruction and soon learn to write reasonably straight. They also learn to make their writing a regular size and to make their ascenders and descenders relate appropriately. For those pupils who experience prolonged difficulty in these respects the use of triple lines may be resorted to as a temporary expedient. A duplicating master for this purpose is included in the Infant Copymasters.

As children develop their mastery of handwriting techniques they can be reasonably expected to write on lines as well as on plain paper. At first they should use wide-spaced (15mm) lines but later this space can be reduced to 8mm. It is common practice as well as simple logic to teach children to use the lines so that the writing 'sits' on the line. The 'x height' should be half of the line width while ascenders should reach up to the line above and descenders reach down half-way to the line below. For formal writing practice it may help to leave a blank line between each line of writing. This will ensure that descenders and ascenders do not overlap.

Towards the top of the Junior School some children may be helped by the suggestion to reduce the size of their writing to occupy ⅔ of the line space. This has the effect, especially when accompanied by a slight slope to the right, of making the writing appear more mature.

The final point to be stressed is that, throughout the years of handwriting instruction, pupils should continue to have some experience of writing on plain paper. Unlined paper has the advantage of allowing the writer to determine the size of writing, spacing arrangement of the page, and the relationship of writing to illustration. It sets the writer free to create an aesthetic whole which enhances the feelings of pride and pleasure. Furthermore, well-formed handwriting is more pleasing against a plain background.

4 Readiness for writing

The factors involved in readiness

It must be accepted that many children will put pencil to paper before starting school and that they may well have been allowed to develop bad habits of pencil hold and/or direction of movement. However, the commencement of formal teaching before children are ready is likely to be, at best, a waste of time and, at worst, positively counter-productive since premature instruction may lead to a sense of failure and frustration which, in turn, may result in tension. Tension associated with failure in learning a skill tends to persist with possibly disastrous effects since success in learning to write depends to a degree on the ability to relax (see p. 25).

The four main factors determining a child's potential for success in learning to write are:

a) motivation

b) motor skill

c) visual perception

d) memory recall

With this in mind, teachers should observe infants as they work and play to ascertain whether they are ready to begin a course of handwriting, and also whether additional activities are necessary to promote readiness.

Motivation

It is important to motivate children to want to learn to write. Even though most young children will come to school expecting to be taught to write it is still necessary to encourage them further by helping them understand the purpose of writing.

1. Attention can be drawn to the function of writing through the display of captions and simple instructions.
2. A variety of purposes for writing can be experienced through role play. The role-play areas of nursery and reception classes, once stereotyped as 'the Wendy house', are now changing environments as creative play is encouraged through a range of imaginative situations. For example, the areas may be set up as shops, cafés, travel agents, railway booking offices, doctors' waiting rooms or estate agents. Teachers involve themselves in the play situations to demonstrate the functions and purposes of writing in connection with real-life activities: designing advertisements, writing menus and filling in forms. Children are quick to imitate these aspects of role play when appropriate materials are readily available. Thus, through deliberately contrived role-play situations, the instinctive development of emergent writing is positively encouraged.
3. When the children co-operate with their teacher in constructing a sentence which the teacher then writes for them as a record of their experience, there are excellent opportunities to demonstrate the purpose of writing and to explain how the writing system works.

Motor skills

Adequate development of fine motor skills can be both observed and encouraged through many activities including the following:

1. modelling with plastic materials e.g., clay, plasticine and dough
2. making 3D models with wood, cardboard, packaging etc.
3. drawing freely or picture making with a variety of media including paint
4. drawing on chalk boards or in sand trays
5. tracing outline drawings
6. joining dots to form pictures
7. following mazes
8. drawing round templates and colouring in outline pictures
9. model making with building bricks, Meccano and other construction kits
10. tracing and copying patterns (pp. 1–15 of the Infant Copymasters provide considerable practice in this).

Visual perception

In a similar manner, adequate development of visual perception can be observed and encouraged through many activities including:

1. sorting and classifying a variety of materials
2. playing matching games with dominoes and cards
3. completing jigsaw puzzles
4. identifying the 'odd one out' in a series
5. reproducing shapes
6. matching pictures
7. matching flash cards from a reading scheme
8. identifying nature specimens etc. by comparing them with illustrations in reference books.

Memory recall

The ability to retain and recall information is an important aspect of learning, and children's abilities in this respect can be observed and encouraged through many activities, including the following:

1. reproducing a simple outline drawing from memory
2. reproducing a sequence of simple diagrams from memory
3. reproducing a sequence of numbers or colours from memory
4. completing an unfinished drawing of a common object
5. remembering the missing item when one is removed from a group.

While many teachers prefer to devise their own exercises for promoting readiness for writing, on the following page are a few examples of activities designed to develop motor skills, visual perception and memory recall.

Other examples of activities that may prove helpful in the preparatory period are included in Part 2 of this manual (see pp. 62–70).

Skipping

Complete the drawings.

Now colour the girls.

Odd man out

Colour him green.

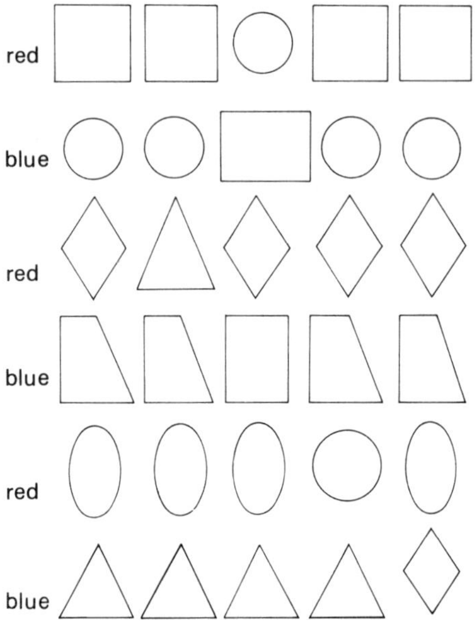

Odd man out

Colour him blue.

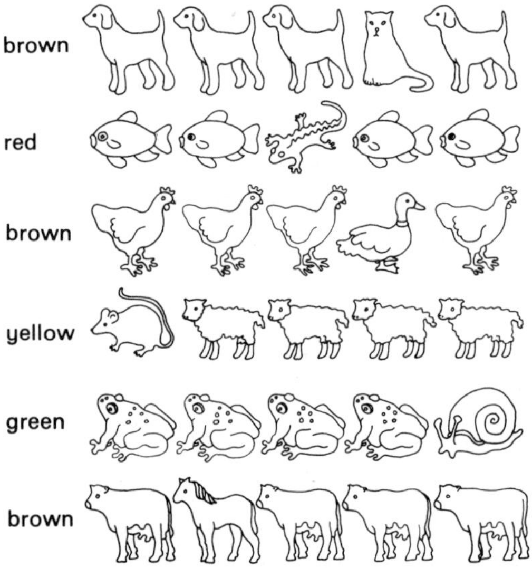

brown dogs   red fish   brown hens

yellow lambs   green frogs   brown cows

Join the dots.

Colour the drawing.

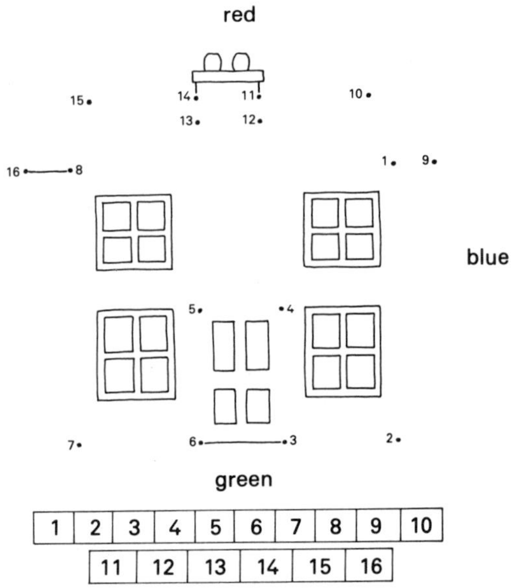

Selected pages from *Keystones 1* by John M. Hughes (Thomas Nelson and Sons Ltd, 1984; First published 1979)

5 The mechanics of writing

Relaxation

The point has already been made that children need to be relaxed in their approach to learning to write. Tension results in early fatigue as well as inhibiting the production of fluent, rhythmic and speedy writing. Harmful tension may arise from an anxiety to succeed or from lack of confidence. It is, therefore, important that the activities designed to promote pre-writing readiness, such as the ones suggested in the previous chapter, are undertaken in a spirit of enjoyment and are free from any element of competition. Everything possible should be done to help children feel relaxed as they practise motor skill development exercises. Miming exercises may prove useful in helping young children to relax their muscles, for example:

a) washing, wringing, rubbing, shaking and folding clothes
b) brushing hair
c) stroking a cat
d) playing a musical instrument
e) playing with snow, bubbles, feathers, balloons etc.
f) picking up sweets to put in a dish.

While more formal tasks designed to promote relaxation could be counter-productive with young children, at the Junior stage pupils can be taught to help themselves by practising relaxation exercises of the following kind:

a) Sit in the writing position but with arms dangling limply. While in this position let the hands flutter loosely.
b) Let the forearms lay limply on the table in the correct writing position. Raise and lower the elbows several times. Raise the forearms slightly with the desk edge serving as an axis, the hands hanging loosely and the fingertips touching the desk.
c) Place the elbows on the table with the forearms held upright. Let the hands flap loosely backwards and forwards while the fingers make slight snatching movements.
d) Clench and unclench the fists repeatedly with the fingers spread.
e) Drum lightly with the fingers on the table.
f) Circle the hands, inwards, then outwards, and then fling them loosely sideways and downwards.
g) Hold the pen in the natural tripod grip lightly (see p. 27). With the forefinger tap the pen or pencil gently.

Posture

Children need to feel comfortable and relaxed when writing. If the table at which they sit is too high the forearm will incline upwards whereas, if the writing surface is too low, the forearm will incline downwards. A table of ideal height supports the forearm so that it rests lightly on the table and is parallel to the floor. Similarly, the height of the chair should be such that the thighs are horizontal and feet flat on the floor. Children should be encouraged to sit up straight with the body slightly inclined towards the table and the elbows just to the side of the body. The left-handed pupil may turn slightly to the right to allow the left arm more freedom of movement.

Correct posture: left-hander

Correct posture: right-hander

Positioning the paper

The position of the writing paper is also important. For right-handed writers the paper should be placed to the right of the centre of the body and should be straight or tilted slightly to the left. For the left-hander the paper should be placed to the left of the centre of the body and it is helpful to tilt the paper slightly to the right.

Correct paper position: right-hander

Correct paper position: left-hander

Remember to ensure that left-handed children sit to the left of right-handers when sharing dual tables. This will avoid clashes over the central space.

Lighting

Direction of light can also be important. It is advantageous for the source of light to be on the left of a right-hander and on the right of a left-hander but it is obviously difficult to arrange for this to be so. Luckily, sunlight does not normally create intense shadows in the classroom, but artificial light can throw disconcerting shadows onto the paper.

Finger, hand and arm movement

At first the child uses large arm muscles when writing. The hand, wrist and fingers should be relaxed but play little part in moving the pencil. Certainly, infants should be discouraged from attempting to write solely by movement of the fingers.

Eventually, however, the arm should serve merely to carry the hand across the page and writing should be achieved by almost imperceptible movements of the fingers and hand from the wrist.

Pencil and pen grip

Paediatricians tell us that, by the age of three, children are capable of adopting the natural tripod grip for holding pencils etc. Unfortunately, as so many teachers know all too well, many children arrive at school already committed to bizarre grips. As soon as possible children should be encouraged to adopt a satisfactory pencil hold which will enable them to write effectively in a relaxed manner and which will not result in problems at a later stage, e.g., when they start to use fountain pens. It would be wrong to suggest that there is a precise method of holding a pencil that must be adopted by all, but there are basic principles which are generally accepted. With these descriptions of good practice in mind, teachers should assess children's writing habits in a realistic and flexible manner and provide appropriate encouragement and instruction.

Right-handers

In the natural tripod grip the pencil is held lightly between thumb and forefinger, about 3cm from the point, with the middle finger providing extra support. The writing instrument should rest on the end joint of the middle finger. The other two fingers rest lightly on the paper along with the side of the hand. It is important that the pencil hold is so light and relaxed that the pencil can be pulled out of the grip easily.

The pen or pencil should point along the line of the forearm to the right of the shoulder at an angle of approximately 45° to the writing line. Similarly, the angle of the writing instrument to the plane of the paper should be approximately 45°

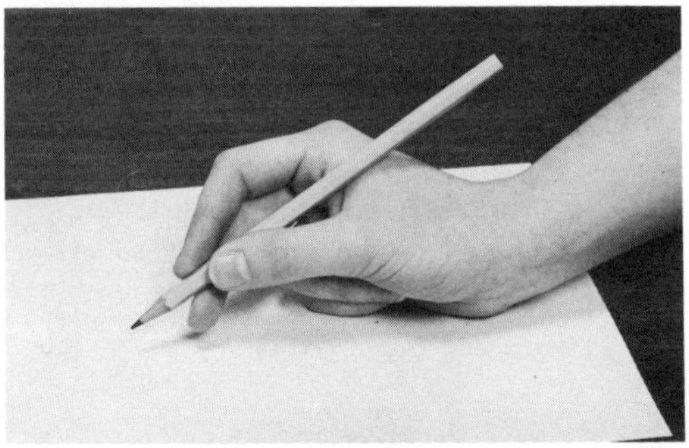

Left. Correct grip: right-hander

Below. Correct pencil angle: right-hander

Left-handers

The method of holding the writing instrument is much the same as for the right-hander except that the grip should be about 4cm from the point instead of about 3cm. This change makes it easier for the writer to see what is written and to avoid smudging ink. Special care is needed to ensure that left-handers do not grip too tightly.

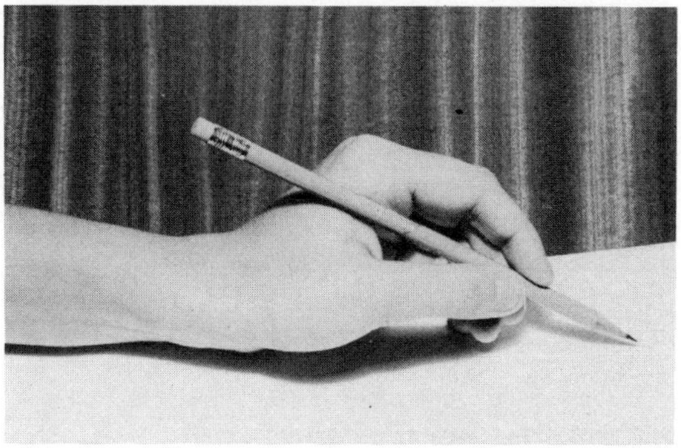

Correct grip: left-hander

Left-handers find the correct angle of pen to paper more difficult to achieve but can be helped through the provision of specially angled nibs. As diagonal joins will involve pushing instead of pulling, it is sensible to ensure that pencils are neither too hard nor too sharply pointed. If pen is being used, the nibs should be rounded and smooth or specially angled.

6 Left-handers

Introduction

Some consideration of the special needs of left-handed writers has already been included in the preceding chapter.

Because of the link between the left to right flow of reading and writing, it is important to encourage children to become committed to one hand or the other for writing. Although the conventions of our writing system clearly favour the right-handed writers, it is generally agreed that it would be harmful to force a child with a strong left-handed preference to change to the right hand.

Determining hand-dominance

The first issue requiring classification is that of 'hand-dominance'. In small children the degree of tendency to use one or the other varies greatly, not only between individuals but also between tasks attempted by an individual. However, most children are found to have developed right- or left-hand dominance for writing by the time they enter school. For those children whose preference is not clearly discernible there is need for careful observation by the teacher.

This whole question of hand-dominance and cross-laterality is discussed at some length in Chapter 7 of *Developing Handwriting* together with suggestions for further reading on the subject.

The following are examples of everyday activities and unobtrusive test situations which may be used to provide clues to likely hand-dominance:

1. picking up a pencil or piece of chalk placed centrally before the child in order to write or draw
2. painting with a paint brush
3. throwing a ball
4. catching with one hand a ball thrown by the teacher
5. holding a bat
6. brushing teeth or hair
7. using a hammer
8. cutting paper with scissors
9. stirring with a spoon
10. screwing a cap on a bottle
11. sorting blocks into boxes
12. threading beads onto a string.

Helping the left-hander

The concern in this manual is to provide good advice for teachers dealing with pupils whose left-hand dominance is both established and accepted.

There are three fundamentals which underlie the help and advice teachers should offer to left-handers:

1. Whereas the arm of the right-handed person moves naturally and easily from left to right across and away from the body, the arm of the left-handed writer is restricted by having to move towards the body. It is important to realise that the natural writing movement for the left-handed writer would be from right to left.
2. It is likely that the left hand, when holding the writing instrument, will move over the top of words being written thus obscuring them from the writer's vision. If the writing was in ink there would be the additional hazard of smudging. When the pen is held 4cm from the point it is easier for the writer to see what is written and avoid smudging ink.
3. When a left-handed writer makes joining strokes it will be with a pushed movement instead of a pulled one as in the case of right-handers. It follows therefore that, if a sharp-pointed writing instrument is used, it will not glide easily and smoothly over the writing surface and may even stick into it. If pen is being used, the nib should be rounded and smooth or specially angled.

Experience shows that when left-handed writers are left to find their own solutions to these problems they are all too likely to adopt unorthodox and unhelpful postures. Consequently it is essential that informed and sympathetic teachers offer positive and systematic help. *Teaching Left-handed Children* by Margaret Clark is a comprehensive work on this subject.

The left-handed children are likely to be aware that they are different from the majority of their fellows, but the teacher should reassure them that they can succeed. The left-hander is likely to find the task of learning to write more difficult than a right-hander but given the necessary extra encouragement and support, left-handers can write just as well as their right-handed peers.

The left-handed pupil may benefit from extra preliminary practice in making large scribble patterns while the teacher observes the techniques involved. A particular problem to watch for at this stage, and when the print script is being learned, is mirror-writing.

Mirror-writing

This phenomenon occurs because of the natural tendency of the left-hander to pull the hand across the body from right to left. Since our writing system, with its left to right direction, does not permit this, the left-hander must push the pencil from left to right.

Mirror-writing is not unusual in young left-handed children and need not cause teachers great concern unless it persists. The majority of children who show a tendency to mirror-write grow out of it by the age of seven or eight. It is, however, necessary to take immediate steps to overcome the tendency and to prevent it becoming a habit.

(Tom Rainbird)

As mirror-writing can only be produced if the pupil starts writing on the right-hand side of the page and then writes from right to left, the following suggestions may be helpful:

1. The practice of marking the starting place with a cross or a coloured margin on the left.
2. An extra emphasis on the left to right direction of conventional writing. The exercises in the Infant Copymasters are all designed to encourage a left to right movement.
3. Slow and carefully directed tracing and copying activities.
4. The use of tactile letters and/or a system of mnemonics, e.g., the Pictogram system in which each pictogram character orients the child correctly by emphasising the writing direction.

7 Fluency, rhythm and speed

Fluency

Fluent handwriting is writing in which the pencil literally flows from letter to letter across the page in a smooth and almost continuous movement. Even single letters should be written fluently.

Although fluent writing need not, necessarily, be very speedily produced, it is not usually produced in a slow painstaking manner. Speedy, regular writing is only likely to be obtained when it is written fluently. Fluency comes from the writer's response to rhythm which, in turn, depends on ease of movement. Hence the importance of posture, pencil hold and relaxed muscles.

Children should be helped to write with fluency and reasonable speed at all stages of instruction but this does not imply that they should be always required to write at maximum speed; they should not normally be pushed beyond their natural rate.

Slow, laboured copying of writing is not an effective method of learning to write. Since the process of writing painstakingly involves different neuromuscular reactions, it does not automatically lead to fluent writing. At all stages of development then the emphasis should be on the acquisition of an easy, rhythmic flow of movement.

Rhythm

Fluent writing is rhythmical in the sense that there should be smooth, steady and continuous movement from one letter to the next, even when the letters are not joined. There should be no unnecessarily jerky or irregular movements and the writer should produce easy, rhythmic and free-flowing movements.

Children are best helped to achieve an easy rhythm by being allowed some freedom to initiate their own movements rather than being forced to conform too rigidly to the form of the model upon which their practice is based. When children reproduce patterns of the kind illustrated below they should be allowed to make free, easy and fluent movements even though their results are only partially correct in the early stages. It is more helpful to reproduce patterns inaccurately but through the correct process than to produce precise copies through laboured, jerky and irregular movements.

Progress towards the desired end of rhythmic joined writing will be aided by an insistence throughout on the rhythm of writing. Most children are familiar with rhythm in singing games, jingles, television advertisements, songs, music and dancing. These auditory rhythms can be used to advantage as accompaniments to rhythmical writing practice. Exercises in the books and in the two sets of copymasters provide appropriate practice in rhythmical movement at various stages. Before children embark on writing these exercises on paper they should learn the movement and establish the rhythm in making it by sliding the blunt end of the pencil over the model or by keeping the point of the pencil just off the surface of the paper. When they are familiar with the movement, the point of the pencil can be lowered and the exercise begun with a 'running start':

Running start

Examples of rhythmic patterns

1. Rhythmic patterns which progress across the page from left to right and are performed to the repetition of a nursery rhyme or to counting:

Jack and Jill went up the hill to fetch a pail of water

2. Straight lines, ellipses etc. made to descriptive naming of the movement, to rhythmical counting or to music:

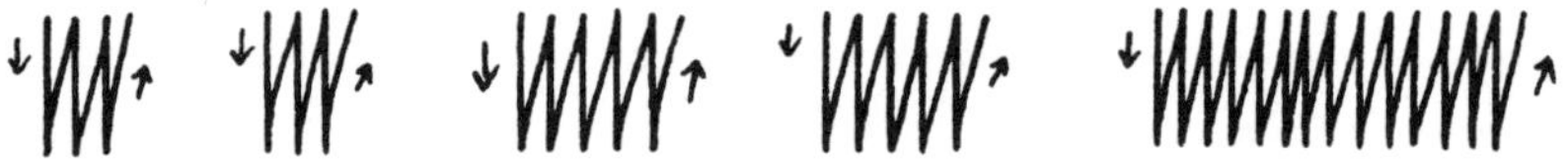

1 – 6   1 – 6   1 – 10   1 – 10   1,2 1,2 1,2 1,2 1,2 1,2 etc.

or   or   or

down up, down up, etc.   down up, down up, etc.   down up, down up etc.

Speed

Although, for normal purposes, slow writing cannot be regarded as satisfactory, speed should not be allowed to appear important for its own sake. As has already been stated in this manual the essential qualities of good handwriting are fluency and legibility. Although fluency will best be achieved at reasonable speed, writing executed at too great a pace tends to lose form, regularity and legibility. There is a deliberate increase in the frequency and fluency of joins in the revised form of Nelson joined writing. This style will now stand up well under pressure as writing demands increase in the secondary school because, when the simple letter forms are linked in a natural rhythmic manner, they retain their legibility even when written at speed.

From the earliest stages, therefore, teachers should try to ensure that pupils write fluently, that is, rhythmically and at reasonable speed. Even though children's movements are slow at first, providing they are rhythmical they should speed up in time.

Speed tests have been provided at various stages (Book 1, page 28; Book 2, pages 11 and 15; Book 3, page 15 and Book 4, pages 12 and 25) and teachers can set more if they wish. These speed tests are not provided to stimulate children to increase their writing speed at all costs; they are provided to help teachers and pupils ascertain the optimum pace for each child at that particular stage of development.

Speed tests are scored by counting the number of letters written in one minute when copying such a well-known sentence as, 'Mary had a little lamb', legibly. Occasional use of such tests will remind teachers of the wide range of ability among their pupils. Although the speed scores in one class may range considerably some guidelines may be set. Most children following Pupils' Book 2 should be able to write 50 letters in a minute, although a few will be able to write as many as 100. Those following Pupils' Book 4 should have a speed of 100 letters per minute or more.

8 The Infant Writing

Letter forms

'The unchangeable significant letter forms which continue to serve our purpose best today are so established within our civilisation that we cannot tamper with them, it is not possible to devise new basic forms: we can only accept what history gives us.' (From *Primary Education*, H.M.S.O., 1959)

A great deal of thought was given to the choice of the particular forms of the 26 letters in the original Nelson scheme and the criteria considered then are still relevant today. The letter forms illustrated in this scheme are the prototypes of our traditional and satisfying forms.

The lower-case letter forms in the revised Pupils' Books are basically the same as in the original scheme. The only exceptions are letters | and † which are given hooks and become l and t.

Similarly, the capital letters and numerals in the revised scheme are little changed. The only variations are: M becomes M with the centre point reaching down level with the two vertical lines; U which becomes U without the additional concluding vertical line; 4 which becomes 4 with the first line being vertical instead of diagonal and 6 which becomes 6 with a closed loop.

An examination of the letter forms below will confirm that:

1. The letters are simple, legible and pleasing.
2. They closely resemble the printed letters found in most early reading books.
3. They are capable of being developed for use in cursive writing without major change.
4. Most of them can be written in one smooth continuous movement, rhythmically and fluently.
5. The bodies of the rounded letters are oval making their formation in one continuous movement more readily achieved.

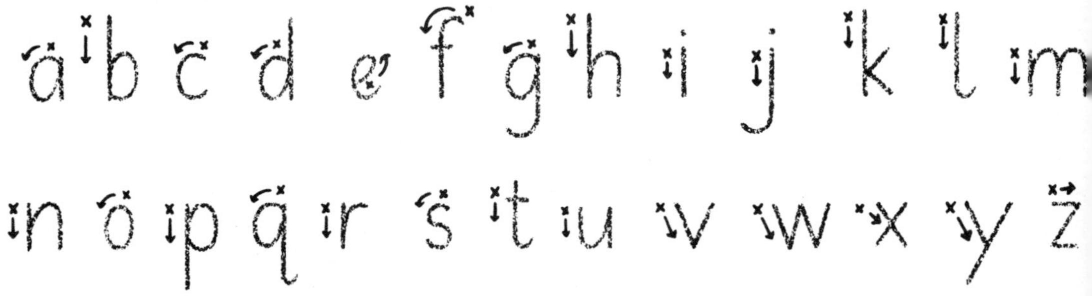

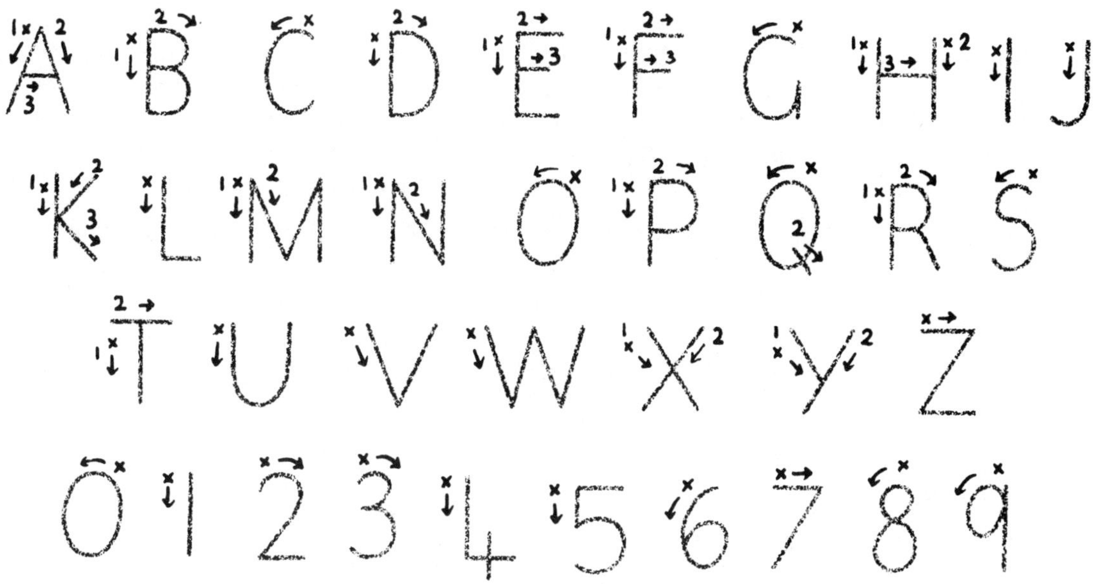

Teachers sometimes have very strong feelings regarding specific letter shapes. It is therefore unlikely that all the decisions made for this scheme will meet with universal approval. When the staff of a school disagree strongly with a particular element of this scheme (for example, perhaps preferring y to y), there is no reason why they should not adopt their preferred form of the letter. There must always be room for flexibility in the use of any scheme but not in a school's policy for teaching handwriting. A policy for teaching handwriting should always be implemented consistently throughout the school (see p. 46) so that children may feel confident when making letter forms.

It cannot be stressed too strongly that easy rhythmical production of writing is of far greater importance than accuracy and uniformity in copying the models in the pupils' books. However, children should be discouraged from major departures from the basic letter forms.

Relative heights and proportions of letters

Ideally capital letters and letters with ascenders should be slightly less than twice the 'x' height and similarly, letters with descenders should be just under twice the 'x' length.

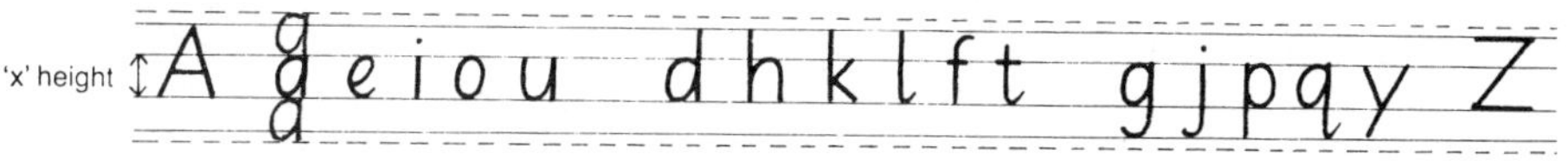

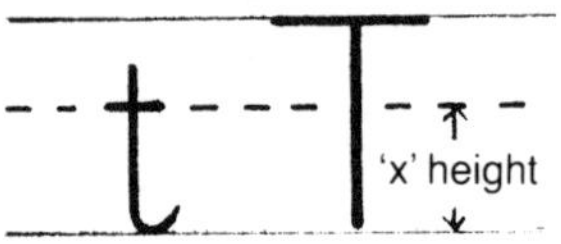

However, very young children cannot be expected to appreciate such fine distinctions and it seems sensible to instruct young pupils to make their letters with ascenders and descenders and their capital letters twice the height of ordinary lower-case letters. They should certainly be discouraged from making ascenders and descenders too long. They should also learn from the beginning to make the letter *t* of intermediate height.

Capital letters vary in width. The generally accepted proportions are shown here for the guidance of teachers:

The cross strokes of *A*, *B*, *E*, *F*, *H*, *K*, *P*, *X* and *Y* all intersect at approximately mid-height of the letter although *A* seems better balanced when the bar is slightly lower.

Spacing

For the guidance of teachers the recognised rules for the spacing of letters are as follows:

jump limit

wide spacing
when two vertical strokes come together

pig hollow

medium spacing
when an oval and a vertical stroke are adjacent

good dog

narrow spacing
when two oval letters are adjacent

It is not recommended that these rules for spacing are taught to children. It is sufficient that they are encouraged to write letters fairly close together so that all spaces between letters look the same. Words should be spaced so that they are distinguishable as parts of a sentence. At this stage, for Pupils' Books A and B, the width of a finger is a satisfactory measure.

This line is too tightly spaced

This line is too widely spaced

This line is correctly spaced

Numerals

The numerals chosen for this scheme emphasise the essential form of each number and are deliberately plain and simple. All numerals are the same size.

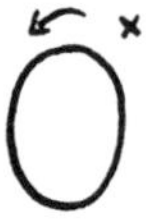
oval – not circular

simple vertical stroke

single curve and straight base

the upper curve is slightly smaller than the lower

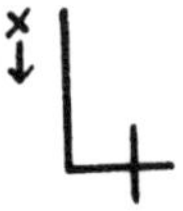
the first stroke is vertical and the cross stroke crosses the horizontal

made by adding the horizontal top last

should be made in an anticlockwise direction and have a closed top

flat top and angular turn

starts at the top with an anticlockwise motion

starts at the top with an anticlockwise motion and is one continuous movement

Techniques for teaching the Infant Writing

Pupils' Books A and B are intended to provide good models for practice and to suggest a possible sequence for teaching. Since these books do not contain any written instructions, teachers will appreciate the need to mediate between the material and their pupils and, in so doing, will make use of teaching techniques in their repertoires. In the page by page commentary which forms the second part of this manual suggestions will be included when appropriate. In this chapter general advice is offered.

The most vital thing to remember is that the acquisition of correct habits of letter formation and good posture is far more important than accurate and precise reproduction of the models in the Pupils' Books. In this connection the over-simplification of Infant Writing into 'ball and stick' cannot be too strongly deprecated. The other essential consideration to be borne in mind throughout the learning stage is the need for pupils to be motivated to be interested in written language, to see purpose in writing and to be confident of their ability to succeed.

Among teaching techniques which have been found to be useful in the early stages are:

1. encouraging children to observe carefully while the teacher writes a phrase or sentence arising from a shared experience
2. drawing attention to the connection between certain letters and the related writing patterns
3. directing children to form letters by drawing in the air
4. tracing over tactile letters with a finger
5. writing over shadow writing
6. drawing round templates (Ensure there is a system for getting templates the right side up and the right way round.)
7. writing in sand with finger or stick
8. writing with chalk and chalkboards
9. writing letters boldly with a candle and applying a colour wash
10. forming letters by arranging pegs on a pegboard or beads in plasticine. (Encourage children to start at the correct place and proceed in the right direction.)
11. forming letters with fingers and/or bodies individually or in groups.

9 The joined style

Changes from the first edition

The revised Nelson style of cursive writing retains the general appearance of the original Nelson joined style but some changes have been made to the frequency and nature of the joins. The other major change is that all rules for correct joining are taught in the first book so that children become committed to the cursive style much sooner and more effectively than was the case in the earlier version of the scheme. It also facilitates the development of individuality, and the emergence of individual characteristics is encouraged in the later books of the scheme. Care was also taken to ensure that the Nelson style develops quite naturally out of the previous print script without undue need for re-learning and modification.

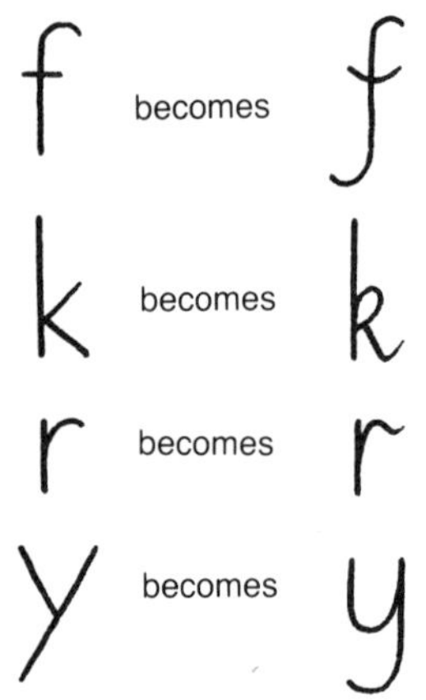

Changes from the Infant Writing

The only lower-case letters which require significant change and, therefore, introduce a small element of re-learning are *f*, *k*, *r* and *y*.

The top of letter *f* should now be at about the same height as the top of the letter *t*. Ample provision is made in Pupils' Book 1 for attention to be drawn to these changes and for the new forms to be practised. Junior Copymaster 8 provides further reinforcement practice.

There is no change to any of the capital letters. The capital letter forms taught in Books A and B continue to be used in Books 1–4 and, of course, they are never joined to lower-case letters.

Joins

The fundamental principle that joins between letters are only worthwhile if they increase the speed, rhythm and ease of writing without reducing legibility underlies the highly logical development of the style. Joins should be made naturally and easily in order to aid the speed and rhythm of writing. In a lengthy word without break letters the teacher need not expect all possible joins to be made since it might be difficult for some children to write such a word in a single smooth, continuous movement without lifting the pen from the page. It is also basic to the scheme to appreciate that the majority of joins are effected through the same easy rhythmical movement that characterises the upswing in the swings pattern:

In view of this emphasis on rhythmical movement when joining letters, the scheme does not include a stage when static entry and exit joins are added to individual letter forms (see Ready Reference, p. 2).

Which letters join?

Joins are made both to and from the following 17 letters:

a c d e f h i k l

m n o r t u v w

Joins are made to but not from the following 8 letters:

b g j p q s x y

Joins are *never* made to or from the letter *z*.

Sets of joins

To assist teachers and children in learning to write the cursive style in a logical and orderly manner the task has been presented in Pupils' Book 1 in five stages. The 26 lower-case letters of the alphabet have been allocated to five sets according to the nature of the joins they require. It is hoped that these simple classifications will make explanations clearer and easier to remember.

Notice that some letters occur in more than one set:

Set 1

The set of lower-case letters which have hooks at the bottom of the 'x' height (see Pupils' Book 1, p. 7).

a c d e h i k l m n t u

Set 2

The set of lower-case letters which are written commencing at the top of the 'x' height (see Pupils' Book 1, p. 7).

a c d e g i j m n o p q

r s u v w x y

Set 3

The set of lower-case letters which are written commencing at the top of the ascender (see Pupils' Book 1, p. 15).

Set 4

The set of lower-case letters which conclude at the top of the 'x' height (see Pupils' Book 1, p. 19).

Set 5

The set of lower-case letters after which no join is ever made (see Pupils' Book 1, p. 25).

Rules for joining

It is possible to teach five rules for joining based on these five sets. The rules are explained and ample practice provided in Pupils' Book 1 (see pp. 7–26). Additional practice and revision exercises are provided in Pupils' Books 2–4.

The five rules are as follows:

Rule 1
(the basic join)

The join from any member of Set 1 to any member of Set 2 is exactly the same movement as the up-swing occurring in the swings pattern.

Rule 2
(the second join)

The join from any member of Set 1 to any member of Set 3 is the same as the basic join except that the join enters the ascender half-way up the letter then continues up to the top of the ascender and then down again to the bottom of the letter.

Rule 3
(the third join)

The join from any member of Set 4 to any member of Set 2 is a shallow horizontal curve because the join is from the top of the 'x' height of one letter to the top of the 'x' height of the next.

Rule 4
(the fourth join)

The join from any member of Set 4 to any member of Set 3 is the same as the basic join except that it goes from the top of the 'x' height of one letter towards the top of the ascender of the next.

Rule 5
(the break letters)

Joins are never made *after* the letters in this set. No join is ever made *to z*.

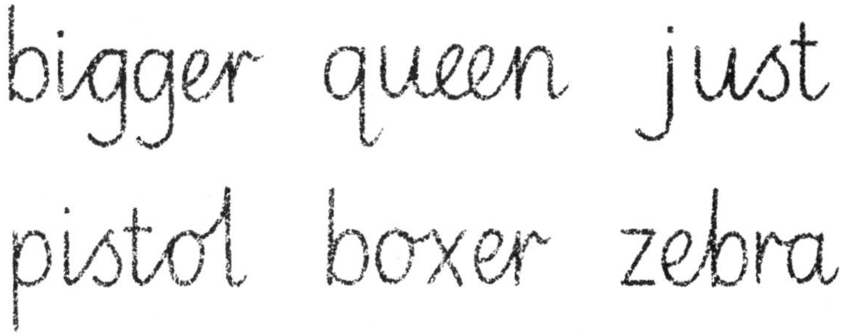

A small space should be left after the break letter so that they are spaced as evenly as the joined letters (see 'Spacing of words and lines' below).

Special cases
joins to *e* and *s*

In practice, the letters *e* and *s* have slightly varying forms because their shapes depend on the nature of the preceding join.

Although these variations may *appear* daunting, in practice they are formed easily and naturally and greatly increase the cursiveness of the Nelson joined style. Attention is drawn to these special cases in Pupils' Book 1 (p. 12–13 and 21–22) and additional practice in writing them is provided in Pupils' Book 4 (p. 9).

Spacing of words and lines

As the size of writing decreases so should the space between each word. At the stage when children are using Pupils' Book 3 this space should be the width of a lower-case *a* and the space between lines of writing should be about twice the height of this letter:

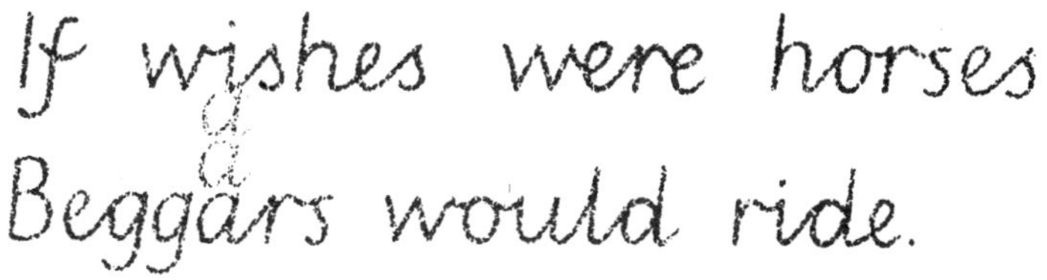

C

Particular care should be taken to ensure that the space after a break letter is not so large that the word appears fragmented:

Techniques for teaching the joined style

Pupils' Books 1–4 have been carefully planned to help teachers decide an appropriate sequence of learning steps and to ensure ample revision. The revised version of the Nelson scheme is organised to accomplish the learning of the complete style in the first year through the use of Pupils' Book 1. The basic teaching technique underlying the work in Pupils' Book 1 is the presentation of the learning task as five categories of join and the way these rules for joining relate to the five sets of lower-case letters. Once the children have been helped to make a careful comparison of the Nelson joined style with the print script, the teacher can begin teaching the rules for joining. It is recommended that this course, which is outlined in pages 7–25 of Book 1, should be covered in a few months, while enthusiasm is high. While they are still learning the rules, children should continue to use the print script for all other written work. Then when all the rules for joining have been thoroughly taught and practised, the children should be encouraged to use the joined style for all writing. Considerable reinforcement practice is also provided in the Junior Copymasters (see page 142).

When considering techniques for teaching the Nelson joined style the most important points to remember are:

1. In the early stages correct movements and fluent rhythms are more important than the appearance of the writing. Children should be discouraged from making patterns or producing writing through wrong techniques even though they manage to achieve results that appear to be satisfactory.

2. Since handwriting, and particularly cursive writing, is a movement skill, it is essential for teachers to provide good demonstrations and then to observe the children while they practise.

3. Most children will need additional practice and, providing they have been taught the necessary movement techniques, models such as those provided in the pupils' books may be used.

In addition to the teaching method outlined above, and developed in the pupils' books and in the second part of this manual, it is expected that many teachers will introduce other strategies to reinforce their teaching and to bring variety to the tasks of their pupils. Such techniques include relating letters to basic patterns:

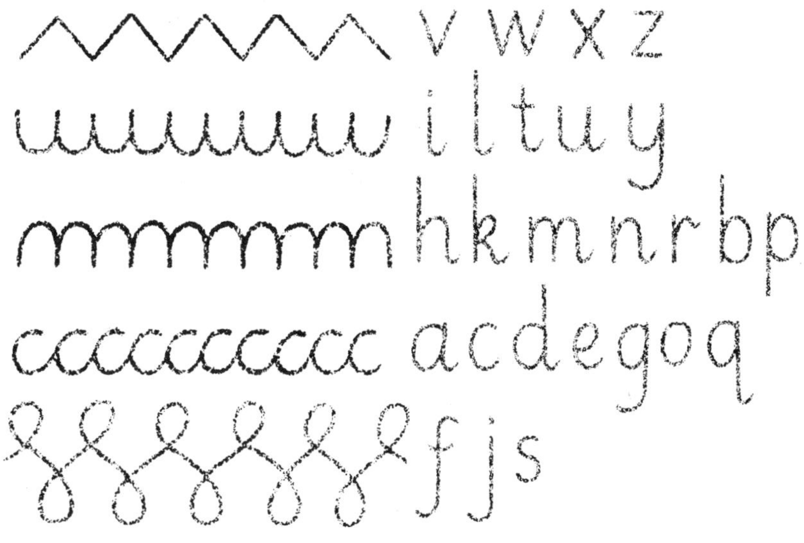

10 Assessing handwriting

The importance of assessment

It is important for individual schools to adopt their own policy for teaching handwriting so that it is taught consistently throughout the school. It is, therefore, vital to involve all members of staff when formulating the school policy so that they will understand it fully and implement it effectively. However, it is also necessary to follow a programme of structured teaching and regular assessment. *New Nelson Handwriting* is designed to provide such a programme and includes recommendations for self-assessment by pupils as well as monitoring by teachers.

Even teachers who have previously given little conscious thought to the question of monitoring progress will have experienced a feeling of pleasure and pride when presented with well-produced written work. Similarly, they will probably have had occasion to require unsatisfactory written work to be redone.

However, while this kind of appraisal is clearly useful and necessary, experience suggests that informal monitoring is insufficient on its own. Too many children have slipped through the net and acquired incorrect habits of movement and letter formation which prove difficult to eradicate later. In those schools where a more structured approach to monitoring has been introduced, teachers have welcomed the periodic reminders to focus on fundamentals. The number of children requiring remedial help at a later stage has fallen correspondingly.

Methods of assessment

Monitoring children's progress requires both observation of children writing and of their finished work. Choice of formal assessment procedures will, of course, vary widely from school to school. Listed below are examples of the kinds of procedures that might be profitably introduced:

a) Termly inspection of examples of each child's handwriting by the head teacher or a delegated colleague, perhaps the language co-ordinator. In some schools an example of each child's normal handwriting is appraised alongside a piece of his/her best work. It is important in carrying out monitoring of this kind to assess each child against his/her own potential, taking care neither to under- nor to over-estimate this. It is also helpful to not general trends within a class/school and to feed back compliments and constructive criticism to teachers. A school exhibition of good examples is a useful adjunct at this time.

b) Termly observation of writing habits in every class in a school, again, initiated by the head teacher or curriculum leader. Each teacher is required, within a given period, to set aside a few minutes when all members of the class are writing to observe carefully the posture, pencil grip and general performance of each child. If a list of names of children with writing problems is drawn up, special help can be provided at an early stage and fewer children allowed to develop fixed bad habits.

c) Objective assessments of the kind discussed above are facilitated by the use of a checklist. A checklist has been prepared especially for use with *New Nelson Handwriting*. It is included in the Junior Copymasters so that it can be easily duplicated. A checklist could be completed for each child and form part of a personal record to accompany the pupil as (s)he moves up the primary school. Alternatively, checklists might only be used for those children with handwriting problems.

Criteria for assessing handwriting

A large part of any assessment of the quality of handwriting is, of course, likely to be subjective. It will depend on many things, not least of all the teacher's assessement of the ability, effort and potential of the individual child. It cannot be stressed too strongly that a child's handwriting should not be rigidly measured against his/her success or failure to replicate the stereotyped calligraphic model contained in the Pupils' Books. One of the aims of this scheme is for children to work towards their own individual style. However, despite this subjective factor there are criteria for assessing the quality of handwriting, and it is one of the objectives of *New Nelson Handwriting* to foster in children themselves an understanding of these criteria. If a child is not to go away with the unhelpful blanket instruction 'to do it better', it is essential that the teacher identifies and explains the particular features that are causing the child difficulty.

At any stage of development the main criteria to be employed in considering a child's work should include at least the following:

- Is it formed with the correct grip and the correct basic movements?
- Is it written fluently and rhythmically?
- Is it legible?

The answers to these questions will, of course, only be found by a close observation of *how* a child writes and *what* (s)he writes. A close observation of a child's writing behaviour should also reveal the reasons for failure.

Significant faults will be discussed in detail in the following chapter, but can be quickly detailed here. They are:

- faulty pencil grip
- incorrect formation of letters
- reversals and inversions
- mirror-writing

Beyond these major writing problems there are a number of detailed criteria for assessing the quality of finished written work. These are reiterated throughout the Pupils' Books but awareness of them in detail should help teachers to focus children's attention on how to improve their performance when redoing work. They are as follows:

- Letters Are their shape and size right?
  Are their slopes right, and consistent?
  Do they have the correct relative height?
  Is the inter-letter spacing appropriate?
- Words Is inter-word spacing appropriate?
- Joins Are they the correct shape?
  Are their slopes correct and consistent?
- Lines Are they straight?
  Is there sufficient space between them?

11 Significant faults: diagnosis and cure

Significant faults and minor deviations

A policy for monitoring progress in handwriting as discussed in the previous chapter should result in faults being perceived at an early stage so that treatment to eradicate them can begin before the bad habits become fixed.

Although there are probably as many 'faults' as there are children, most of these faults are fortunately nothing more than minor deviations from standard practice. Teachers need not be concerned about deviations from the norm which do not prevent the child learning to write acceptably. The descriptions of 'good' practice in this manual are not intended to be prescriptive, and it is only those bad habits which hinder present performance or which might lead to difficulties later in the child's development that require remedial attention.

Significant faults are, on the whole, bad habits of performance which will mainly be diagnosed by watching children write, although a close scrutiny of finished writing will often reveal the fruits of such difficulties.

Particular problems and solutions

Among the most common faults that require attention are the following:

1. Faulty pencil grips

Many small children grip their pencils too tightly so that their muscles are too tense and they have difficulty in producing rhythmic smooth writing. An over-tight grip is the commonest faulty pencil hold. Crooking of the forefinger is often a sign that the pencil is held too tightly. It may also be revealed by the undue pressure and heaviness of finished writing. The cure is to make the pupil hold the pencil with the thumb and middle finger and merely rest the forefinger on the pencil.

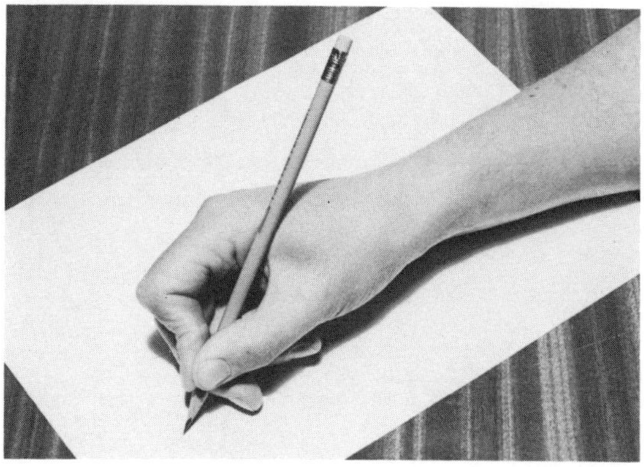

Over-tight pencil grip

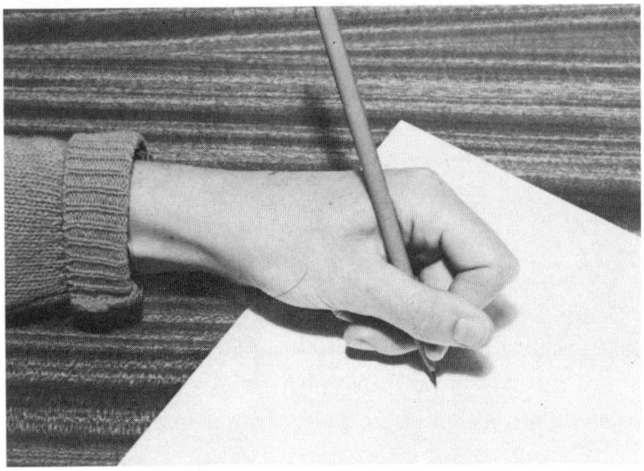

This grip will lead to two problems: cramping of the muscles as writing demands increase and smudging when the grip is transferred to other writing instruments such as fountain or felt-tipped pens.

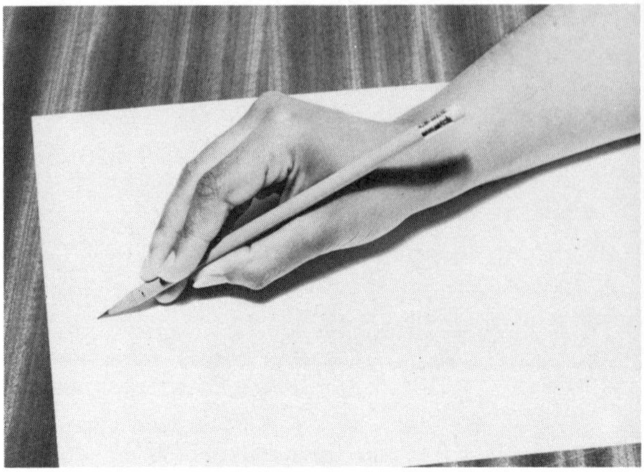

The middle finger should not rest on the pencil as this may reduce fluency of movement and lead to undue pressure on the paper when writing.

These photographs show two other pencil grips that will lead to difficulties in handwriting.

2. Incorrect formation of letters

Forming letters incorrectly at the print script stage will lead to difficulties in joining later. It is important to explain this to children because to them these faultily drawn letters will look indistinguishable from those formed correctly.

Incorrect letter formations will be most easily detected by watching children write, but a close study of children's finished work may reveal tell-tale signs of error.

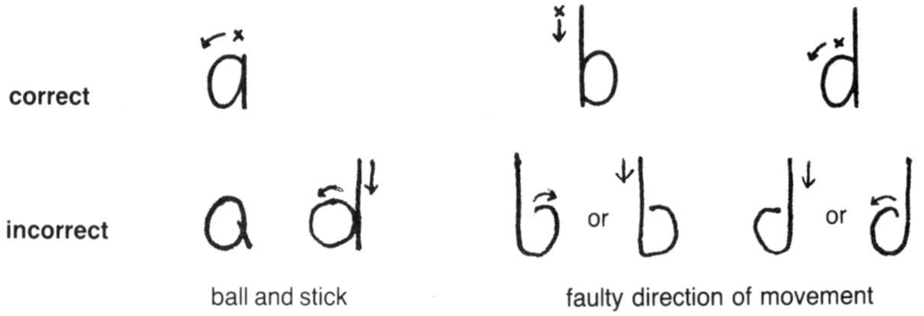

The most common and troublesome error arises from the practice of forming the letter *o* and its related letters as a clockwise circle:

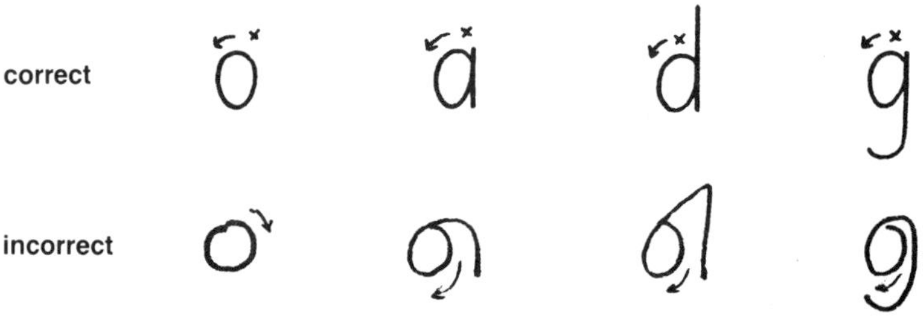

The problem can be remedied if these letters are seen to develop from *c* and its related pattern.

Incorrect letter formations can be most easily analysed by looking at the letters in groups and relating them to the patterns from which they derive.

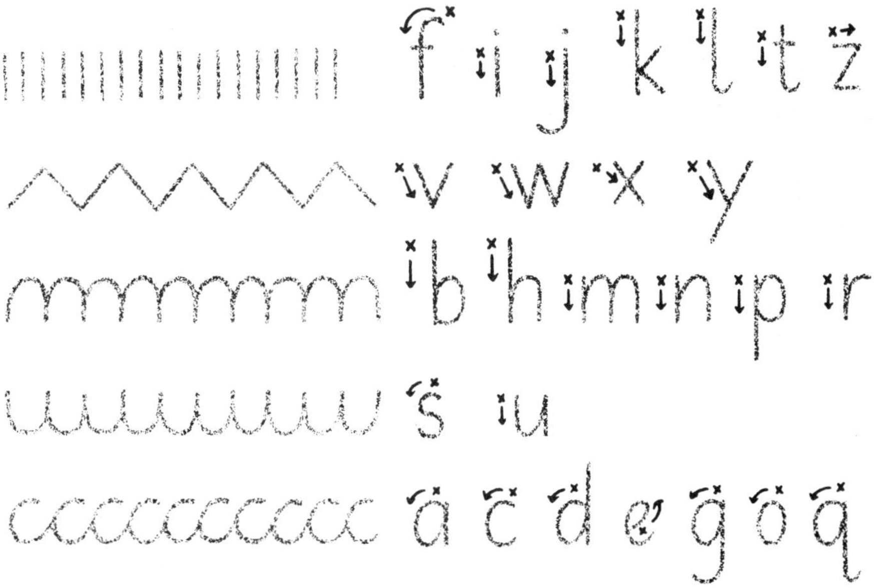

The development of good habits of letter formation is greatly helped by preliminary work on the basic patterns which are fundamental to correctly made letter forms.

In cases of doubt over letter formation, asking a child to copy out a complete alphabet would be a useful diagnostic exercise. Junior Copymaster 7 is useful for this purpose.

3. Reversals and inversions

This fault is certainly not uncommon and results in children writing *b* for *d*, *p* for *q*,*w* for *m*, *saw* for *was* and *pat* for *tap* etc.

'plum' with reversed *p* 'pie' with inverted *p* 'doll' with reversed and inverted *d*

The underlying cause of this problem may be confused laterality, lack of commitment to one hand or merely general immaturity, and the majority of children do overcome the tendency by the age of eight. These children can be helped through emphasis on the writing direction, through encouragement to become consistent in their use of one hand for writing and through training in visual discrimination.

4. Mirror-writing

This phenomenon, which is more common in left-handed children than among right-handers, has been discussed in the chapter on left-handers (see p. 31)

Underlying problems

1. Lack of confidence

Since children need to be relaxed when learning to write, any tension or anxiety induced by problems at home or in school may impede their progress. Indeed some small children actually enter school with a degree of emotional anxiety about their apparent lack of success in handwriting while others become anxious because of their experience in school. It is just as important that neither parents nor teachers induce anxiety through over-critical demands on their children as it is to try to help them avoid acquiring bad habits. Provided that children are allowed to develop the necessary skills at their own pace but with appropriate instruction and support there are few children who cannot achieve satisfactory progress.

2. Specific learning disability

The term *dyslexia* is sometimes used in connection with children with specific learning disability, but the term continues to be controversial. None the less, when children of apparently normal or superior intelligence and general ability find great difficulty in learning to write they should be carefully diagnosed and, if necessary, referred to an educational psychologist.

General strategies for corrective teaching

1. Demonstrations and instruction

One way of helping children overcome faults is through the provision of additional and repeated demonstrations and instruction along the lines suggested in the sections on teaching techniques (see pages 15, 40, 41, 46). Such additional practice may well be best organised for individuals and small groups so that close supervision is possible.

2. Use of mnemonics

Many children find that mnemonics help them to focus on and retain the shape of letters and correct methods of forming them. Over the years many teachers have developed mnemonics to help pupils but perhaps the most highly developed published system available is *Pictograms*. The Pictogram system was developed by Lyn Wendon and is especially helpful for children with learning difficulties as it uses verbal instructions which are entertaining, concrete and specific.

3. Use of audio visual aids

Children experiencing difficulty in learning to write require the support of repeated advice and as teacher contact time is so precious it can be helpful to utilise audio-visual aids for this purpose, for example:

a) A workcard or worksheet appropriately illustrated can be accompanied by a commentary recorded on a cassette tape so that a child may practise the exercise repeatedly.

b) A more sophisticated method of achieving the same end is through the use of a Syncrofax Teaching Machine. Programmes for use with this machine are produced on a special A4 sheet which has a four minute recording disc on the back.

c) An overhead projector can also be used to provide further variety in the teaching of handwriting. It has the advantage of allowing the teacher to face the class while demonstrating.

d) The potential of the computer as a teaching aid providing instant feedback has yet to be fully investigated in relation to handwriting.

4. Programmed learning

Another approach to the treatment of handwriting problems is described in *Preventing Classroom Failure* by A. Ainscow and D. A. Tweddle. They have developed a series of programmes designed to help an individual child or group of children achieve specific goals. A step-by-step learning programme is constructed, based on a careful assessment of what a child can, and cannot do. The child's performance is then measured at the end of each stage in the programme to ensure that an acceptable degree of accuracy within a reasonable amount of time is being attained.

12 Improving standards

New Nelson Handwriting provides regular revision exercises but, in addition, it is important that teachers regularly monitor the writing standards of their pupils and, when necessary, set appropriate exercises to be redone. It is, moreover, also necessary to give thought to ways of motivating children at all stages to at least maintain and, preferably, to improve their standards of handwriting.

The first essential is that teachers clarify their own position in this respect and consider refraining from making perpetual hollow appeals for pupils to do 'best' writing even when the occasion does not warrant 'best' writing and the teacher has no intention of enforcing the demand. It is more helpful to expect children to write with a reasonable degree of care at an appropriate speed for most normal purposes so that their writing is legible and fluent but not too painstakingly produced.

'Best' writing is surely best reserved for those occasions when attention can be concentrated on the mechanical skills of writing and when there is seen to be a purpose for producing aesthetically pleasing work. It is often helpful to point out to children that practice in writing a conscious 'best' hand should result in a gradual improvement in their work when writing at normal speed. Older children should be helped to realise that some writing tasks require a draft version be written first. Then, after revision and editing, the draft can be re-written in 'best'.

Most of the writing undertaken at normal speed in primary schools occurs in the process of practising language skills, recording and describing experiences or experimenting with creative uses of language. For these purposes, when pupils are primarily concerned with composition, vocabulary, spelling and punctuation etc., it would be unreasonable and unnecessary to expect 'best' handwriting. However, many opportunities to encourage aesthetic presentation of written work arise naturally in the classroom or can be contrived. The suggestions which follow have been found useful:

1. an annual or termly handwriting competition arranged, perhaps, by the appropriate post-holder
2. the permanent allocation of a noticeboard on which frequently changed exhibitions of good writing are displayed
3. writing out work for wall display in connection with thematic work etc. after rough drafts have been corrected
4. re-writing letters after rough drafts have been corrected, especially if the letters are actually written to be sent, and not merely as classroom exercises
5. a personal anthology of poems, literary extracts etc., compiled individually

by each child who should be encouraged to make the writing, illustration and decoration beautiful so that it matches the choice of contents

6. where an occasional class or school magazine is duplicated for circulation, a handwritten version can be produced by the children writing out their own contributions in their best writing
7. producing handwritten, decorated programmes etc. for school plays and bazaars
8. the decoration of work with bands of well-made writing patterns
9. encouragement to experiment with different ways of presenting writing:
   a) shaped writing where the writing is arranged so that the space it occupies forms a shape which relates to the subject
   b) curved or spiral writing as a change from conventional straight lines
   c) elaborating and decorating capital letters
   d) the use of coloured inks
   e) writing over illustrations which have been only lightly coloured
   f) experimenting with the relationship between writing and illustration rather than following the all too common arrangement of writing followed by the picture

13 Exercises, patterns and designs; effective practice

Pre-writing practice

Young children delight in scribbling and drawing and this informal play develops control over the writing instrument. In nursery and reception classes opportunities should be provided for free experimentation with a wide range of writing instruments on a variety of surfaces. Children can also be encouraged to colour in the spaces between the lines they draw and to fill in outline drawings carefully. As children enjoy these early informal activities, teachers should observe them and help them to acquire good writing habits. It is never too early to consider influencing children to hold their pencil correctly and lightly and to pencil lightly with relaxed and easy movements. As their skill develops, a point will be reached where formal instruction can begin (see Chapter 4: Readiness for writing).

Patterns at the Infant stage

Pupils' Books A and B begin with several pages of suggestions for practice in making useful movements freely and rhythmically. Such exercises further develop control and other good writing habits. The first half of the Infant Copymasters contain invaluable further practice.

Examples of exercises for use in the early stages:

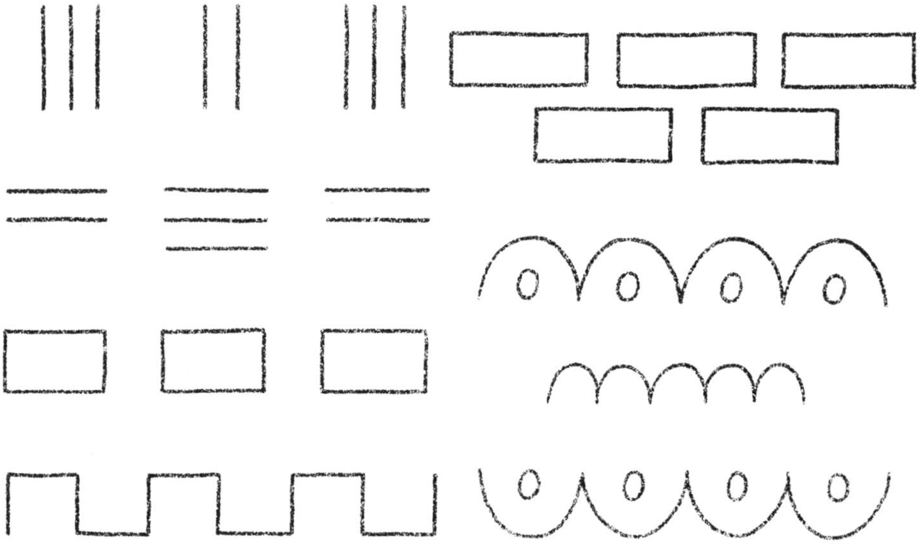

Patterns at the Junior stage

The more complex exercises included in the Junior books practise movements used in letter making and joining, encourage the development of control, and emphasise the need for regularity and consistency. At this stage it becomes obvious to children when their patterns do not 'work' because of unevenness.

Examples of these more complex exercises:

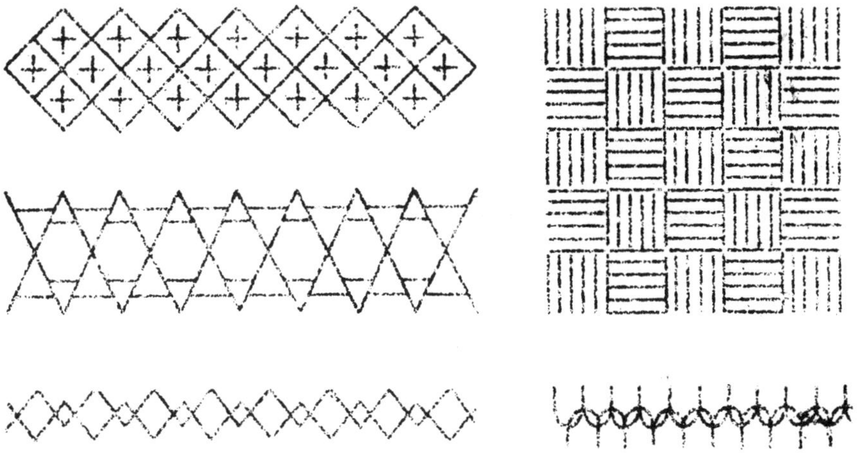

Exercises are provided at every stage of the course and in both books of copymasters. Junior Copymasters 3–6 will be found particularly valuable at the Junior stage.

Patterns made from rows and combinations of letters provide practice in using the writing instrument and in making letter forms. Children should be encouraged to practise the patterns illustrated throughout the Pupils' Books and to devise their own. Strips of pattern derived from letter strings and then coloured appropriately make an excellent decoration for work of various kinds.

Care must, however, be exercised when children make writing patterns. It is all too easy for letter forms and joins to deteriorate if patterns are undertaken too hurriedly or carelessly. The prime purpose in encouraging children to produce these patterns is to provide effective practice in good writing habits.

Effective practice

While it may be true that improvement in a motor skill such as handwriting comes with practice, teachers must beware of the old adage – 'Practice makes perfect!' Indeed, if children are allowed to practise over a lengthy period of time without conscious endeavour to improve, there is a danger that their performance may become established at that level. Aimless practice of handwriting without supervision by the teacher can be positively harmful. Adequately motivated and properly directed practice is needed for real improvement. Here is a summary of the principles for effective practice that have been identified in this manual:

1. Pupils must be helped to feel that it is important and worthwhile to improve their writing. They should be encouraged to strive consciously to do so each time they practise.
2. Practice either of a formal or informal kind must be purposive, meaningful, interesting and enjoyable. The feelings that accompany the acquisition of a skill are important.
3. Teachers should observe *how* children write and make frequent checks on the quality and fluency of their writing. Improvement in performance will be retarded no matter how hard pupils try if their writing techniques are faulty.
4. Pupils need a clear understanding of how they can improve their writing. They should be given precise guidance as to the most effective methods of doing so.
5. Practice will sometimes be directed to the achievement of a clearly defined and specific goal, e.g., the correction of a faulty pencil hold or the correct formation of a certain letter or group of letters.
6. There is a need for frequent short formal periods of instruction and practice in handwriting as distinct from the many occasions when writing is done in the service of other subjects and purposes.
7. When pupils are writing stories or exercises their main concern should be the content rather than the mechanical skill. However, the improvement in handwriting resulting from the formal periods of instruction should be reflected in the quality of their writing produced in other lessons.
8. Children should be helped to learn to recognise and, in time, to measure their standards of performance. Improvement in a skill is more likely to continue to increase if the performer is able to recognise rises in level of achievement.

Part 2

Using the Pupils' Books and the Copymasters

Preparing for Pupils' Book A

Introduction

Although the concept of readiness for writing is also discussed in Chapter 4 of the first part of this manual, the topic is important enough to warrant further coverage.

As children entering school vary widely in physical and mental development, not all will be ready to profit immediately from formal instruction in handwriting. Fortunately, the programme of activities normally provided in nursery and reception classes presents teachers with ample opportunities to observe children and to encourage them to undertake tasks that will help promote readiness for writing.

The most important task for teachers in connection with children's writing in the early stages is to take positive steps to ensure that the children appreciate the functions of writing. Teachers who make a practice of telling their pupils about the writing that they have been doing themselves and about letters and postcards that they have enjoyed receiving are clearly contributing to awareness of the importance of writing. However, it will also be essential to provide opportunities for the children to observe their teacher actually writing. Attention can thus be focused on aspects of the writing process in an unthreatening manner.

Many opportunities to write for the pupils in a purposeful manner occur in a busy nursery or reception classroom. The list would be endless but includes:

records of collaborative composition
records of personal experiences dictated by pupils
captions for classroom friezes or models
wall stories
organisational notices to announce rules, etc.
instructions for games
thank you letters
greetings cards
menus and recipes

During the preparatory period teachers should also:

a) observe their pupils and assess their abilities and stages of development

b) determine the hand preference of each individual pupil (see p.30)

c) provide play activities and exercises to develop control of larger muscles:

throwing, rolling, catching and bouncing balls; skipping; dancing; running and jumping to music; climbing on agility apparatus; hammering; games and play activities involving large arm movements such as pretending to be windmills or the branches of trees in the wind.

d) Provide activities to exercise the smaller muscles of hand and fingers and to develop co-ordination of hand and eye:

folding paper; cutting out shapes; recognising geometric shapes and fitting them into frames; model making with large plastic Meccano and other constructional toys; building and stacking with bricks; using screw toys and pegboards; modelling with clay, plasticine and other malleable materials; drawing in sand; scribbling and drawing on chalkboards and blackboards with chalk or on large sheets of paper with paint brushes, felt pens or jumbo crayons; playing with tactile letters and jigsaw puzzles; games and miming involving finger and wrist movements.

e) give miming exercises to relax muscles:

washing, wringing, rubbing, shaking and folding clothes; brushing hair; stroking a cat; playing a musical instrument; playing with snow, bubbles, feathers, balloons etc; picking up sweets to put in a dish.

f) give initial guidance towards correct pencil hold and helpful posture (see pp. 26–28).

g) provide pre-reading activities that relate to learning to write:

activities to develop visual perception such as jigsaw puzzles; matching games; classification of geometric shapes and other sorting materials; reproduction of shapes by drawing or modelling; matching pictures; matching letter, word and phrase flashcards; identifying differences.

h) give practice in writing movements using paint brushes, felt pens, chalk and, finally, thick pencils. The sequence for these activities might well be:

1. undirected scribbling movements
2. simple directed movements and rhythmical pattern exercises involving letter elements
3. for some pupils, copying meaningful words, phrases and sentences. (The emphasis should be on ease and rhythm of production and the feeling of the movement when writing, rather than on excellence of form produced.)

A sequence of preparatory writing activities

The following is a sequence of writing activities which teachers might like to use to lead in to Book A:

1. writing movements using paint brushes, felt pens or chalk
2. scribbling exercises with pencil
3. recognising shapes and filling in outlines with coloured pencils
4. rhythmic writing exercises to counting, music and rhymes
5. writing movements with pencil making elements of letters, figures and patterns
6. copying of letters, words and sentences

The exercises which follow under these separate headings are not intended as a rigid scheme of work which must be followed. Rather they are to be regarded as suggestions to the teacher as to what may be attempted according to the size of class, the ability of the pupils, the size and nature of the classroom and the availability of materials. These exercises are not substitutes for opportunities for free expression and experiment with media and materials. Directed activities of this kind should be viewed as preliminary activities to formal handwriting.

Stories might be woven around each exercise, no matter how simple, to give it purpose and to add to the child's pleasure in the activity. Where possible, children should be encouraged to become independent by collecting their own materials and returning them to the correct cupboard at the end of the lesson.

1. Writing movements using a paint brush

a) Bridges, or boy hopping, etc.

Clockwise movement – up – over – down. *Relaxation exercise*: making bridges in the air with wrists and fingers relaxed.

b) Waves on the sea or skipping

Relaxation exercise: arms making swaying movements up and down.

c) Climbing up and down mountains

Relaxation exercise: with the muscles of the arms, wrists, and fingers loose, flap hands up and down.

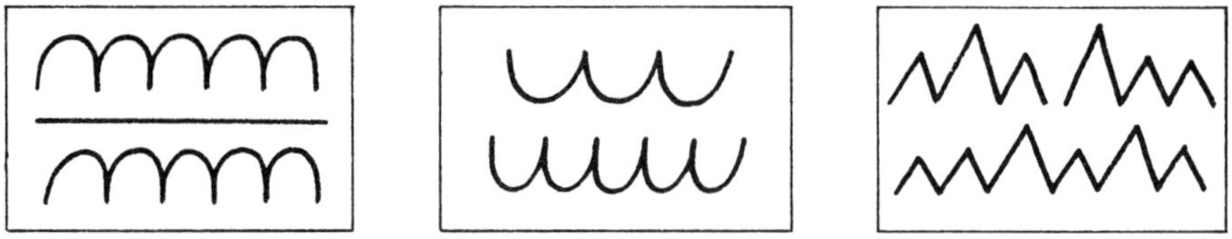

a　　b　　c

d) Snakes and ladders

Show children how to fill page with curves of various colours and sizes. Add ladders if desired. *Relaxation exercise*: arms hanging loosely from the shoulder, let hands and fingers flutter limply.

e) Coloured Easter eggs in a box

Paint eggs of various colours with coloured bands round them. *Relaxation exercise*: with elbows resting on the desk, rotate hands from the wrist.

f) Pattern

Show children how to fill the page with a pattern of ovals and straight lines.

Relaxation exercise: with fingers loose, pretend to play the piano on the surface of the desk.

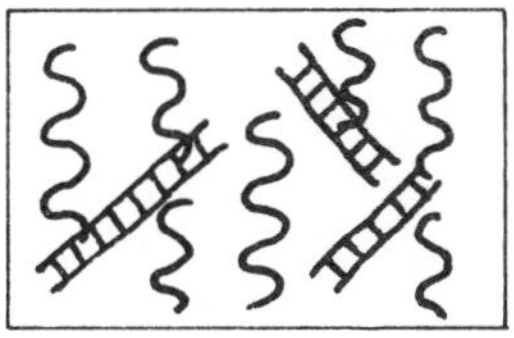

d

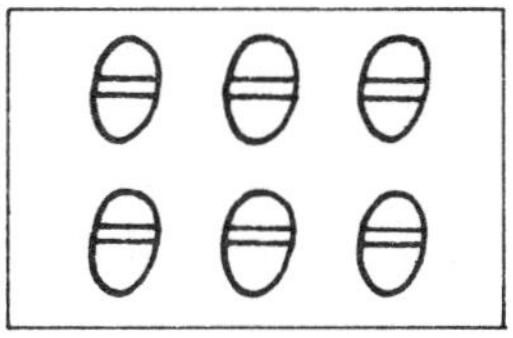

e

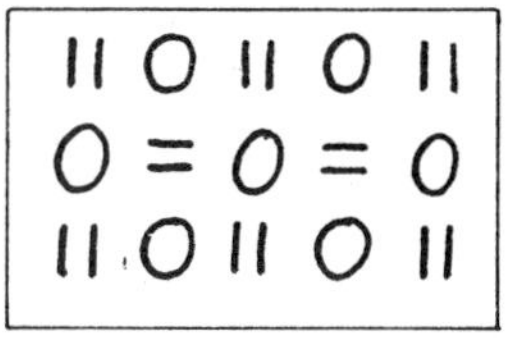

f

2. Scribbling exercises with pencil

A pencil with a thick soft lead should be used and the child taught how to hold it lightly in a reasonably correct manner. The exercises should be done on sheets of cheap blank paper such as newsprint, and each exercise should be performed many times. The child should be allowed to scribble freely and rhythmically to gain confidence and practice in using the new tool correctly.

A relaxation exercise can as usual precede each scribbling exercise.

Exercises such as the following can be devised:

'Smoke from a bonfire'. Draw a small pile of sticks to represent a bonfire and fill the page with scribbles to represent smoke. The important aspect of the exercise is how it is performed rather than the quality of the finished product.

In a similar manner pupils may make scribbling lines to represent clouds, dust billowing from behind a vehicle, waves and spray, a fountain playing, waterfalls and rapids, a ball bouncing or rolling, a piece of paper blown by the wind, fireworks, a wheel turning.

An exercise which will be enjoyed by the children is commonly known as 'taking the pencil for a walk'. The pencil makes a continuous line as in the diagrams below.

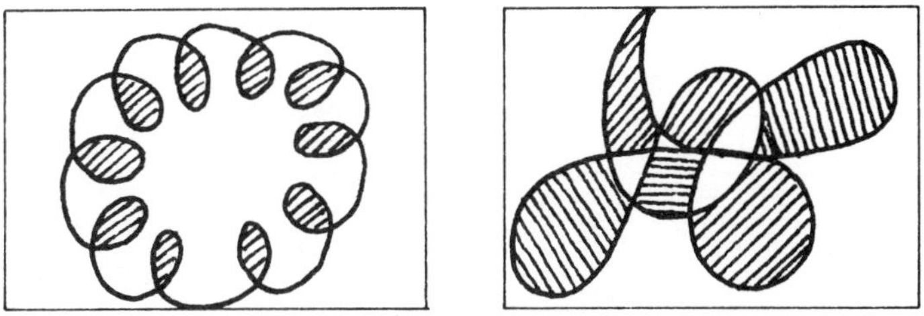

taking the pencil for a walk and shading the enclosed shapes

The enclosed spaces can be shaded in with crayons of various colours to make an attractive pattern.

3. Recognising shapes and filling in outlines

Natural materials such as leaves, together with sensory apparatus such as Montessori insets, wood and cardboard shapes and profiles of trees. Flowers, leaves, animals, letters and numbers which are normally found in infant classrooms can be used with advantage at this stage. Children handle these materials and move a finger round the edge to feel the shape. They are then provided with sheets of cheap paper and pencils, crayons or coloured pencils with which they draw round the shape. The outline thus drawn can then be filled in with coloured pencil. When one outline has been filled in, the children may be allowed to choose other insets and fill their paper or a page of their large writing books with coloured shapes. Children should not be asked to trace round small or intricate shapes, nor should they be allowed to use small stubs of crayons or pencil.

4. Rhythmic writing patterns to music, rhyme or counting

Children who have performed the exercises detailed in the earlier sections should now be beginning to sit correctly when drawing and writing and be better able to use a pencil in a reasonably satisfactory manner. Attention must now be placed increasingly on the ease and rhythm of writing. The following exercises will give pleasure to a child and help to impress on him/her the need to move his/her pencil smoothly and steadily when (s)he writes. The teacher must recognise that in the early stages it is more important to watch the writer and how (s)he writes than it is to pay attention to the end product.

These exercises can be used with advantage at all stages of instruction throughout the school. The Pupils' Books contain many additional examples.

a) Rhythmic patterns which progress across the page from left to right are performed to the recitation of a nursery rhyme or to counting. The five patterns illustrated below give practice in making all the movements used in writing.

Jack and Jill went up the hill to fetch a pail of water, etc.

Mary, Mary quite contrary, etc.

Humpty Dumpty sat on a wall, etc.

Hickory, Dickory, Dock, etc.

One two, buckle my shoe, etc.

The exercise can also be performed to a steady repetition of 'one, two,' where the downstroke is made on the count of one and the upstroke on the count of two. If a rhyme is used, each stroke can be associated with a monosyllable but a very precise metrical correspondence need not be sought. As long as the children say the verse steadily and write fluently and rhythmically as they repeat the words, the purpose of the exercise will be served.

b) Straight lines, ellipses, letters and patterns performed to descriptive naming of the movements, to rhythmical counting or to music.

Up, down, etc, or 1, 2, 1, 2.

The simplest of these exercises is the repetition of a straight up and down movement on one line. This type of exercise can be performed to the naming of the movements, to counting or to music. It will be found to be particularly useful in helping children to develop a sense of rhythm in making writing movements. The exercise, illustrated here, of running a pencil or the finger continuously up and down against a straight edge such as a book, board or ruler, will be found helpful particularly with the less able children. These exercises should be performed frequently for short periods at a time until the child can make the movement speedily, confidently and rhythmically.

The exercise can then be varied by making the strokes to a specific count or by allowing the strokes to progress across the page:

1–6 1–6 or down up, down up, etc.

1–10 1–10 or down up, down up, etc.

1,2 1,2 1,2 1,2 1,2 1,2 etc. or down up, down up etc.

Exercises such as these can be made to a count of one for each separate stroke up or down or to a count of one for each combined up and down stroke, depending on the speed and rhythm with which the pupils are able to write. The aim is to maintain a steady, rhythmical movement. Similarly for the continuous ellipses illustrated below it will be necessary to adjust the count according to the size of the ellipse, the skill of the pupils and the tempo desired. Thus in the earliest stages, each ellipse may have to be made to a count of four or to a naming movement such as *over*, *down*, *round*, *up*.

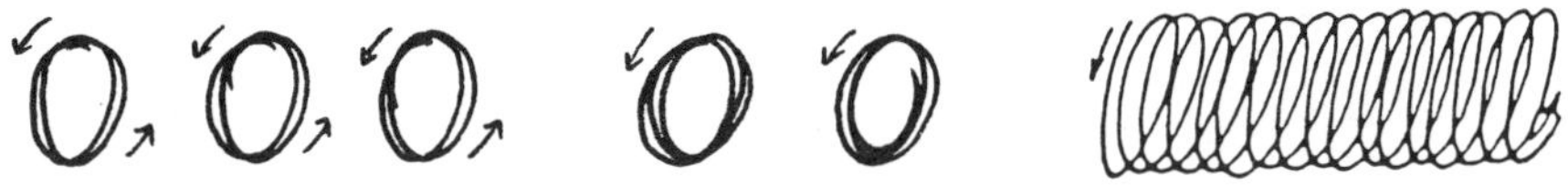

1,2 1,2 1,2 for each ellipse or down up, down up, etc.

1–10 or down, down, etc

1–10 or down and down, etc

complete ellipse for each beat

It should be borne in mind that the establishment of a fluent, rhythmical movement rather than precision or excellence of form must be the first objective. Before the children write on paper, they can learn the movement and establish rhythm in making it by writing with their fingers in the air or on the desk, or by sliding the blunt end of their pencils on the desk or paper. When they are familiar with the movement, the pencil can be lowered and the exercise begun with a 'running start'.

On occasion, exercises such as those illustrated in this section may be performed to music with a well-defined beat, but as there is likely to be a wide variation in the natural rates and rhythms of individuals in the class, class exercises to music should be used with discretion and not as the sole method of instruction.

As the children's skill grows, they may attempt more difficult exercises such as those on the page following which, although appropriate to the Junior stage, may nevertheless be found to be both enjoyable and profitable.

Running start

Linked letters

5. Writing movements with pencil

The emphasis in the exercises in the preceding sections has been on the rhythm and feel of the movement involved. Now, there must also be an increasing attention to improvement in the form of what is produced. In the exercises which follow, a more precise and restricted movement is demanded than formerly. It should be remembered that these exercises do not serve their purpose if the child is allowed to draw very slowly, carefully, heavily or jerkily. Each exercise should be repeated many times with increasing speed, rhythm and freedom of movement. The writing of letter forms should grow easily and naturally from these early free writing activities. It is always sound practice to associate the exercise with familiar objects or movements or to present it in the form of a story, e.g., swings, waves, fences, dress patterns, decorations for books or Christmas cards, toys, animals, etc.

Some of the exercises of this type are illustrated below.

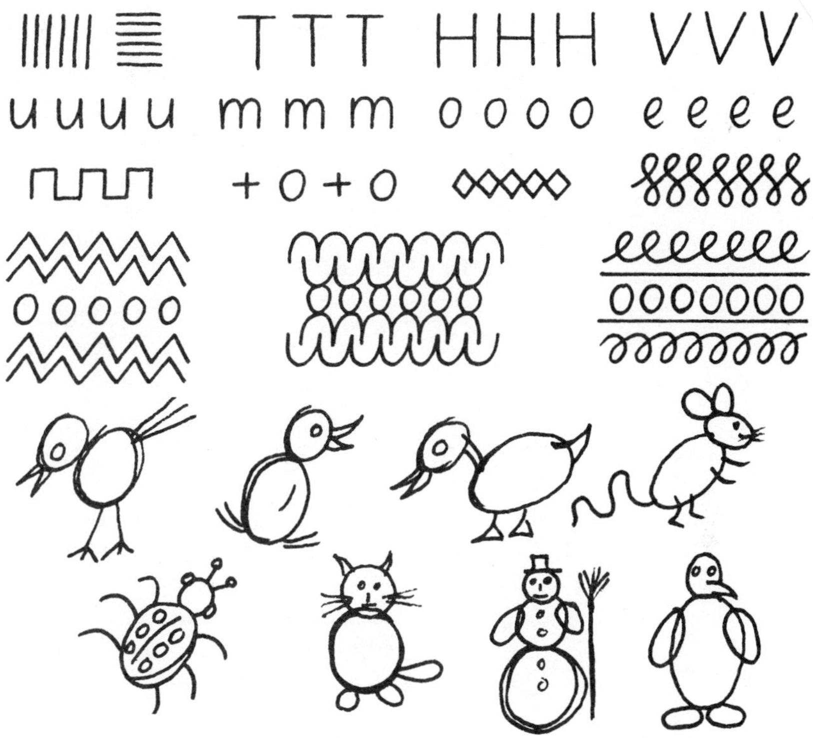

Pupils' Books A and B and the Infant Copymasters contain many more examples. Many of the simpler shapes can be combined to make attractive patterns which will delight the child, especially if colour is used for part of the pattern or to fill in the spaces enclosed.

6. Writing letters, words and phrases

Since handwriting is a mechanical skill, it should be based on sound mechanical principles. Exercises, such as those described above and elsewhere in the scheme, are necessary for the efficient and satisfactory development of the skill. Practice in making letters with occasional casual instruction is unlikely to give the amount or kind of practice required to achieve the degree of skill required.

However, it must be remembered that handwriting is also a means of expression and of communication so children should be motivated to want to write words and phrases from an early stage, certainly before they can possibly have been taught the correct ways to form all letters. It follows therefore, that during the preparatory period, children might make some of the letters by an incorrect series of movements. No lasting harm should result from this, especially if teachers use the many opportunities that will arise to teach children correct methods as soon as possible. The teacher's priorities should be:

1. to stimulate the desire to write and encourage children to write freely and rhythmically in a size appropriate to their degree of neuromuscular development

2. to help their pupils acquire satisfactory writing techniques and to guard against the formation of habits that might lead to problems later

The stage should then be set for formal and systematic handwriting instruction which is sequential and cumulative, along the lines discussed in the remainder of this manual.

Formal instruction

There need be no sharp distinction between the preparatory and formal stages and many of the exercises recommended for the preparatory stage might usefully be used throughout the Infant stage and well into the Junior stage although the children would be expected to perform the activities with increasing fluency and skill as they mature.

Readiness

Formal instruction in the correct methods of forming letters is probably best left until the child is ready to begin to learn to read and has had some experience of written words and phrases. Indeed, every effort has been made throughout this scheme to ensure that models provided for writing practice are of interest to the pupils and that, whenever possible, they also help to develop their knowledge and understanding of the intricacies of the English writing system.

Grouping

It is probable that, in the early stages of formal instruction, teachers will work with groups of children judged to have reached the same stage of readiness. Teachers should find the advice which follows helpful in preparing their lessons. The suggestions relate specifically to pages in the Pupils' Books and are arranged in the same sequence. However, teachers are reminded that, if they think it advisable, exercises may be undertaken in a different order to meet the needs of particular groups of children.

Materials

Writing materials are fully discussed in Chapter 3 of Part 1 of this manual but teachers are reminded that early formal practice is probably best undertaken using:

a) a thick stemmed soft-lead pencil or a standard pencil as preferred

b) blank paper, although some children may be helped by folded or ruled lines which divide the sheet of paper into three or four bands

The children then write within the areas so created but *not* on the lines. As children's skills improve they may prefer to write in large books (e.g., 30 × 30 cm) which contain only a few sheets of plain paper. Then, as children's skill improves still more, the page size might be reduced and the number of pages in a book increased.

Posture

Although undue insistence on correct posture and pencil hold can be discouraging, it is important that good habits are established as soon as possible. Acceptable techniques are described and illustrated in Chapter 5 of Part 1 of this manual but teachers are reminded of the following key points:

1. ensure that each child is seated at a table and chair suited to his/her stature.
2. encourage children to sit correctly:
   a) feet flat on the floor
   b) body bent forward slightly
   c) head up from the paper and not turned to one side
   d) elbows off the table
   e) hands and arms able to move easily
   f) paper in front of the right side of the body for the right-hander and the left side for the left-hander. (See Chapters 7 and 8 of Part 1 of this manual.)
3. Encourage children to hold their pencils correctly in the natural tripod grip. The following routine has been found helpful in encouraging good writing habits and can be adapted for use by the left-hander:
   a) lift pencil with the left hand
   b) hold right hand in a writing position with muscles relaxed and forefinger slightly curved
   c) place the pencil between the thumb and forefinger in the correct writing position and hold it very lightly about 3 cm from the point (4 cm for the left-hander)
   d) let the middle finger rest lightly on the pencil
   e) hold the pencil very lightly and take care not to press heavily on the paper when writing.

When giving guidance of this kind, teachers must avoid over-insistence on precise adherence to rules as this could result in tension. As relaxed muscles are needed for efficient handwriting techniques, tension is to be avoided.

Pupils' Book A

Contents

Pupils' Book A covers the following:

- Preliminary exercises to develop neuromuscular co-ordination, fluency, rhythm and quality of movement
- Systematic instruction in all 26 lower-case letters in letter families
- Introduction of familiar words to write
- Introduction of simple pieces of continuous writing

List of contents

Further practice of some of these items will be found in the Infant Copymasters. Relevant copymasters for further practice are indicated in brackets. A full chart cross-referencing the Infant Copymasters to Pupils' Book A will be found on p. 141)

Page by page guide

Page 1

The purpose of these exercises is:

1. to provide material for practice while instruction is given on correct posture and pencil grip
2. to give practice in moving the pencil fluently and rhythmically with a definite purpose.

The teacher can introduce each exercise by drawing on a blackboard while the group watch. The children then practise the exercise several times until they can perform it satisfactorily. While the children are practising, the teacher should circulate and help pupils who adopt unsatisfactory postures or who hold or use the pencil in an unsatisfactory manner. The emphasis should be on smooth and rhythmical movements. Although great speed is unnecessary, slow, laboured movements should be discouraged.

Suggested movement patterns:

1. Make the large oval first for the body, then draw the head, then the arms and finally the legs. Encourage the children to make each oval in one bold movement starting at one o'clock and moving in an anticlockwise direction. Remember that the quality of movement is more important than perfection and uniformity in the end products.
2. Again, start at one o'clock with a rhythmical anticlockwise circular movement and proceed without lifting the pencil from the paper. The resulting pattern could be likened to the path of a bird in the sky.
3. Make the nests starting at one o'clock and drawing continuously several anticlockwise ovals for each nest. Then add five eggs.
4. Draw each series of matches as a row of vertical lines. Start each one at the top.

Pages 2–4

The exercises on these three pages give practice in making the more precise and controlled movements which are the basis of movements used in writing. If possible, try to associate each exercise with a familiar activity. The exercises should be practised several times until the children can perform them fluently, rhythmically and fairly accurately. Music or counting rhymes often aid the development of rhythm.

The teacher might introduce each page by demonstrating on the blackboard. The children should be encouraged to observe the detail and the movements involved very carefully. The left to right and continuous nature of some lines of pattern should be emphasised and children encouraged to reproduce them without lifting the pencil from the page if possible.

Pages 5 and 6

These pages are designed to emphasise the correct movement for forming the oval shape which is the basis of letters *o*, *a*, *c*, *d*, *g* and *q*. These ovals should all be made in an anticlockwise direction starting from the one o'clock position.

Page 5

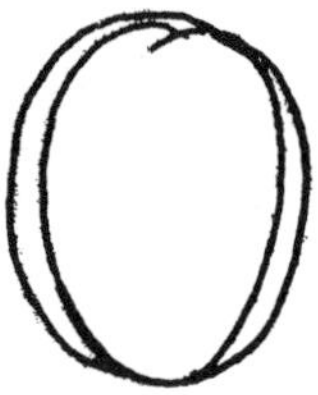

1. Make sure the line of continuous ovals start at one o'clock and are made with a continuous anticlockwise movement. Some children may be aided by rhythmical counting as they draw. Children should practise this movement frequently on loose sheets of paper until they can form the ovals rhythmically and accurately.
2. The other ovals, including those used in simple figures, should all be made in one continuous movement.

Page 6

1. The straight line patterns should be drawn continuously from left to right. A rhythmic chant of *up*, *down*, *up*, *down* etc. may aid the achievement of a regular, uniform zigzag pattern.
2. The ovals should all be made in a continuous anticlockwise movement starting at one o'clock.

Page 7

The *c* pattern

This is the first pupil page specifically devoted to letter formation and may well provide the basis for several lessons. The family of letters based on the oval shape is introduced through the *c* pattern. This pattern is not easy to produce and many children may need to be shown how to make it as a line of separate *c*'s before they are able to make it as a rhythmical flowing line. The pattern is, however, very useful in the development of good movement habits for writing and, ideally, is produced as follows:

Starting at one o'clock, swing back, round and over to the beginning of the next *c*. Then back round again and so on in one continuous movement.

A sequence for teaching this pattern might be:

1. Demonstrate the *c* pattern on the blackboard.
2. Encourage the children to draw it in the air etc.
3. Encourage practice on large, cheap paper.
4. If necessary, demonstrate the alternative pattern, i.e., non-continuous lines of *c*'s:

5. Children may then draw the pattern in their writing books.

The letter *o*

The next exercise on this page is a line of letter *o*'s. The children should be reminded that letter *o* is an oval shape before they write the line of *o*'s in their writing books.

The letter *c*

This letter should now present little difficulty. During blackboard demonstration emphasise starting at one o'clock and finishing directly below. Encourage control, and regularity of shape and size but remember that the process is still more important than the end product at this stage.

The letter *a*

Demonstrate the relationship between *c* and *o* and show how *a* is formed by the same basic movement with an additional vertical down-stroke to finish. Emphasise the importance of writing letter *a* in a smooth continuous movement without lifting the pencil from the page.

The letters *a, c, o*

The letters are presented in random groups to encourage observation of fine difference together with controlled movement when reproducing them accurately.

Page 8

The letter *d*

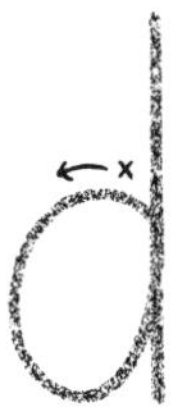

First the *c* pattern is revised to reinforce good movement habits and to establish that letter *d* is also related to letter *c*. The letter *d* should be made in one smooth continuous movement starting at one o'clock, swinging round the oval part of the letter and on up to the top of the vertical stroke and then down again. Children should be advised that the oval part of the letter is about half the height of the whole letter. Teachers should be on guard against excessively large or small vertical strokes but should avoid being over-fussy about precise proportions. The term *ascender* might be introduced here.

The letter *g*

Letter *g* is another single stroke letter which should be made in one continuous movement commencing from one o'clock. The tail should be approximately half the total height of the letter and should not be too curly. The term *descender* might be introduced here.

Words from *c, d, o, g*

Now that these four letters have been taught and practised it is possible to introduce the words *cod* and *dog* which are made from them. Throughout

Pupils' Book A, care has been taken to include only words which can be illustrated to ensure that children understand any words they are asked to write.

Page 9

The letters *a, c, d, g, o*

Once these five letters have been introduced it is advisable to spend a few lessons revising them and their basic pattern. As the children repeatedly practise each letter and the words that may be derived from them they should be closely observed. The following aspects should receive priority:

1. the form of the letters
2. the speed of writing
3. the rhythm of writing
4. good writing habits in general

Page 9 contains letters and words as models for this purpose.

Page 10

The swings pattern

The aim of this page is to provide continued practice in achieving the rhythmical, fluent movements underlying handwriting. The *c* pattern is further revised and the swings pattern is introduced. This pattern is important not only because it introduces the letter *u* but, at a later stage in the development of Nelson handwriting, it is the basis of the cursive joins. The swings pattern should be made continuously and rhythmically from left to right.

Children who find difficulty in persevering across the whole line should be allowed to break the flow as necessary.

Each pattern exercise should be performed many times with a view to improving the rhythm, quality and speed of the exercise.

Page 11

The letter *q*

The letter *q* also derives from the *c* pattern. It should be demonstrated by starting at one o'clock with an anticlockwise oval leading into a vertical down-stroke. It terminates with a short curved upward flick. The descender should be approximately the same length as the height of the oval. The letter should be written rhythmically as a single, continuous movement.

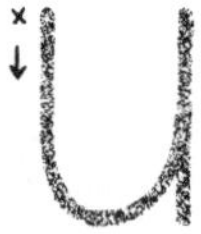

The letter *u*

The swings pattern introduced on page 10 should be revised. The relationship between the swings pattern and letter *u* should be discussed and the children taught that letter *u* is one swing plus an additional vertical down-stroke made in a continuous movement.

Page 12

The letter *e*

The letter is an important one and children often find it difficult. It is advisable to provide several lessons, if necessary, to ensure that it can be made rhythmically, speedily and correctly. Letter *e* is unique in that it starts at the centre and moves upwards, although from then on it follows the conventional anticlockwise oval direction of the *c* family.

Plenty of practice of this pattern will be helpful in establishing correct movements:

Page 12 provides models of the pattern, the letter and the following illustrated words for the children to base their practice on: *egg* and *cage*.

Page 13

The letter *s*

This is another difficult letter to write and preliminary practice with tactile letters etc. will help. Many teachers relate the letter *s* to the wriggle of a snake and any such mnemonic that helps children cope with the change of direction of the curves in letter *s* may prove useful. Demonstration on the blackboard should establish that the starting point and first movement is the same as for letter *c*. Plenty of practice in making snake shapes and the letter *s* on large sheets of cheap paper should precede work in the writing books. Models are provided as a basis for practice on Page 13.

The letter *f*

Demonstration by the teacher should establish that this letter also commences at one o'clock and that the curve at the top is similar to the beginning of the letter *s*. The cross-stroke is a straight line made from left to right at the same height as the top of small letters such as *a* and *o*. Attention should be drawn to the question of height. The vertical down-stroke should extend down to, but not beyond, the writing baseline. The height of letter *f* in print script approaches the height of other letters with ascenders.

Three words incorporating letters *s* and *f* but avoiding any letters not so far taught are illustrated. The children should enjoy copying the pictures and practising *safe* and *sad face*.

Page 14

Revision of *e, f, q, s, u*

These five letters are revised together with their related patterns. Teachers should observe their pupils as they undertake this revision which aims to improve the form of letters and the speed and rhythm of writing. Any children revealing fundamental problems of any kind should be given individual guidance and, if necessary, be taken back to the appropriate page to repeat initial practice.

The words chosen for practice only include letters already learned: *goose*, *case* and *sofa*.

Page 15

Straight line patterns

The exercises provided on this page help to prepare children for writing the letters *l*, *i*, *t*, *j* and *k*. They also give practice in making the precise and controlled movements required in handwriting. Children should carefully observe the teacher's blackboard demonstration of the various patterns. The following points should be stressed:

1. The vertical strokes should always be made from the top downwards.
2. The horizontal strokes should always be made from left to right.
3. All strokes should be made boldly and rhythmically.
4. All strokes in a group should be of equal length and equally spaced.

The simple drawings involving straight lines at the bottom of the page provide additional practice. Children can create their own drawings and designs from straight lines.

Page 16

The letter *l*

This letter should present little difficulty other than the possibility of the curved flick at the base of the vertical downstroke being exaggerated or made too angular. The model on page 16 should serve as a guide when demonstrating. The letter should be vertical and of the same height as other letters with ascenders.

The letter *i*

This letter should be very easily learned. It is just a vertical line the same height, (i.e., 'x' height) as other ordinary lower-case letters. The dot should be placed at the correct distance, vertically above the line before the next letter in the word is written.

Three words incorporating these two letters and others already learned are illustrated: *log*, *lid*, and *flag*.

Page 17

The letter *t*

This letter is made from two strokes. The first is very similar to the letter *l* and the second is similar to the cross-stroke on letter *f*. Letter *t* is intermediate in height between letters with ascenders and the letters of 'x' height. When demonstrating this letter there is an opportunity for the teacher to emphasise that it is the only ¾ height letter. The cross-stroke is a horizontal line made from left to right, before the next letter is written and at the same height as the top of ordinary lower-case letters.

The letter *j*

This letter begins at the top at the same height as other ordinary letters without ascenders. The straight vertical line then continues down below the writing base line into a descender which curves in exactly the same way as letter *g*. The letter *j* should be dotted immediately after it has been written.

The two illustrations at the foot of the page introduce the words *little jug* and *tall jug*, and provide additional practice.

Page 18

The letter *k*

The pattern at the top and bottom of page 18 revises straight vertical lines and introduces diagonal strokes. Children should observe the teacher's demonstration carefully and notice how both upward and downward diagonal strokes start from the same point with the upward stroke being made first. Three strokes are therefore necessary when writing letter *k*. This is to prepare for the eventual conversion of k to k for the joined script.

When demonstrating, teachers should point out that the point on the vertical line where the diagonal lines meet is a quarter of the way up from the bottom. Letter *k* should be the same height as other letters with ascenders and the two shorter legs should reach up to the top of the 'x' height and down to the writing baseline respectively.

Some children are helped by being taught to construct this letter in three dimensions with strips of plasticine, wood, straw or Meccano. The models on page 18 of the Pupils' Book are useful for practice, and three words are illustrated for further work: *clock*, *cake* and *gate*.

Page 19

Revision of letters *i*, *l*, *t*, *k* and *g*, *j*, *q*

The four straight line letters and three letters with descenders are revised on this page. The pictures illustrate the meaning of the words *quick jet*, *kite*, and *lift*. As the children work at this revision exercise to improve the forms of letters and the speed and rhythm of writing, the teacher should watch for significant problems. Children revealing faults should be given individual help and be taken back to the appropriate page if necessary.

Page 20

Bridges and other patterns

The patterns and exercises on this page are designed mainly to give practice in clockwise oval movements in preparation for teaching *b* and *p*. The bridges pattern is very closely related to letters *h*, *m*, *n* and *r*.

These patterns should be demonstrated on the blackboard and practised freely by the children, for instance on large sheets of paper, before more controlled practice in their writing books is required.

The ovals should be made in a clockwise direction in contrast to those made in connection with the *c* family. The open spirals and bridges should be made rhythmically and, as far as possible, continuously from left to right.

Page 21

The letter *b*

Even after ample practice of the patterns provided on page 20, this letter may well cause many pupils considerable difficulty. When demonstrating, it is important to emphasise the following points:

1. The letter starts from the top at the same height as other letters with ascenders.
2. The letter commences with a straight down-stroke to the writing baseline followed by a continuous movement back up almost to the mid-point of the vertical line. There the pencil branches out to form a clockwise oval, finishing back almost at the bottom of the vertical line.

The letter *p*

Letter *p* requires very similar treatment to letter *b* except that the starting point is different:

1. The letter starts from the same height as ordinary lower-case letters (i.e., from the 'x' height).
2. The letter commences with a straight vertical line which extends beyond the writing baseline to form a descender. The pencil then moves back up the vertical line almost to the top where it branches out into a clockwise oval which rejoins the vertical line at the level of the writing baseline.

Three words are illustrated on this page to provide additional practice: *bat*, *bag* and *pipe*.

Page 22

The letter *n*

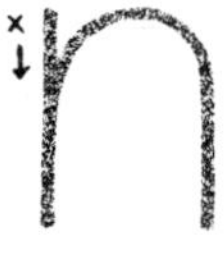

The letter *n* can be thought of as the basis of *m*, *h* and *r* and it also relates directly to the bridges pattern. Once the letter *n* is thoroughly taught and learned the three related letters will be easily mastered.

The teacher's illustration of *n* should emphasise the following:

1. The starting point is at the same height as other ordinary lower-case letters.

2. The letter commences with a vertical line down to the writing baseline. The pencil moves back up the vertical line almost to the top where it branches to form a curved arch and concludes with another vertical line back to the baseline.
3. The letter should be made in one continuous movement.
4. The width of the letter should be the same as *a* or *o*.

The letter *m*

The letter *m* is made in almost exactly the same way as the letter *n*. The one important difference being that when the pencil reaches the writing baseline at the conclusion of the first arch it should move up again to form the second arch in one continuous movement. The pencil should not be lifted from the paper during the course of writing a letter *m*. The letter *m* will, of course, be much wider than a letter *n* – almost twice as wide.

Three words are illustrated on this page: *nose*, *nut* and *man*.

Page 23

The letter *h*

The teaching procedure is much the same as for letter *n*. For letter *h*, however, the starting point is at the same height as the top of other letters with ascenders. The vertical line is made down to the writing baseline at which point the pencil moves back up the vertical line to almost the mid-point. The pencil then branches out to form an arch which concludes with a final vertical line. The width of letter *h* is the same as that of letter *n*.

The letter *r*

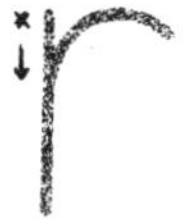

The instructions for teaching letter *r* are identical with those for teaching letter *n* except that, when the pencil branches right to form the arch it is lifted before the end of the arch is reached.

The words *hen*, *car* and *rabbit* are illustrated.

Page 24

Revision of letters *b*, *p*, *n*, *m*, *h* and *r*

The bridges pattern and the family of six related letters are revised on this page. Five illustrated words provide meaningful practice of all letters so far taught, but particularly these six letters. The main aim of this revision should be to improve the form of the letters and the speed and rhythm with which they are written. As the children do these revision exercises, the teacher should observe them, provide individual help and, if necessary, take children back to an appropriate page to overcome specific problems.

The words illustrated are: *mother*, *apple*, *bun*, *bell* and *pram*.

Page 25

Letter *w* and continuous prose

Diagonal stroke patterns were introduced and practised on page 6. They should now be revised and attention drawn to their relationship with the letters *w* and *y*.

This brief prose extract from 'The Tale of the Three Bears' has been used here for three reasons:

1. It is likely that the story will be familiar to most children.
2. Apart from *w* and *y* all the letters involved have been taught and practised.
3. The only capital letters included (*W* and *S*) have the same forms as their lower-case equivalents.

The teacher should first read the piece aloud while the children follow it in their books. Next, the children should watch carefully while the teacher writes the piece on the blackboard. As the teacher writes, the opportunity should be taken to reinforce correct methods of forming letters. Attention should also be drawn to such matters as size of letters, alignment of writing (particularly ascenders and descenders), and spacing of letters, words and lines of writing.

Then the children should practise writing the extract in their writing books and illustrating it. As usual the emphasis should be on the correct movements and rhythm of the writing together with pleasure in achievement and interest in the meaning. Not all children will be able to produce neat and accurately formed print at this stage. Those children who need extra practice should be encouraged to repeat this exercise.

Page 26

Diagonal patterns

The exercises on this page mainly involve diagonal lines. Several of the patterns are designed to be produced smoothly and rhythmically. As the teacher demonstrates these qualities the need for continuous movement from left to right should be emphasised. Children may find that practice to counting or music aids successful production of the patterns which should be performed many times, on large sheets of cheap paper to begin with, and then later in their writing books, until the required movements are made confidently and accurately.

Page 27

The zigzag patterns and letters *v* and *w*

The zigzag patterns should be made continuously and rhythmically.

The letter *v*

The letter *v* should be made in a continuous, smooth movement starting from the top and without lifting the pencil from the paper. It is the same height (i.e., 'x' height) as other ordinary lower-case letters. Letter *v* should be the same width, at the top, as the letter *a*.

The letter *w*

This letter must also be made in one continuous movement, starting from the top, and without lifting the pencil from the paper. The letter *w* should be the same height as *v* and almost twice as wide.

Three words are illustrated: *van*, *waves* and *wigwam*.

Page 28

The letters *x* and *y*

The pattern at the top of the page and other patterns involving diagonal lines should be practised to improve rhythm and speed in producing diagonals.

The letter *x*

The letter *x* is made with two separate strokes. The first starts at the same height as the top of the 'x' height and moves diagonally and downwards from left to right. The second stroke commences from the same height but moves downwards from right to left crossing the first stroke at the centre. As the teacher demonstrates, the balance of the letter around the centre should be emphasised.

The letter *y*

At the print script stage, the letter *y* is made by two strokes. The first is identical with the first stroke of letter *x*. The second stroke of *y* starts from the same height as the top of ordinary lower-case letters but moves downwards and diagonally to meet the first stroke at its base on the writing baseline to form a descender of the same length as *g*, *j* and *q*.

Four words are illustrated on the page to provide additional practice in writing *x* and *y*: *box*, *fox*, *boy* and *yacht*.

Page 29

The letter *z*

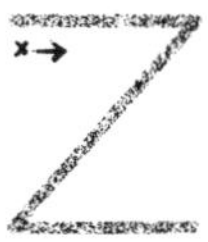

This letter is made in one continuous movement without lifting the pencil from the paper. The starting place is at the top of the 'x' height. The movement is horizontal from left to right and downwards diagonally to the point on the writing baseline immediately below the starting point. The final movement is from left to right along the baseline.

Four words are illustrated for practice: *zoo*, *zebra* and *lazy boy*

Pages 30 and 31

Numbers, numerals and words

The children will have encountered the twenty-six letters of the alphabet

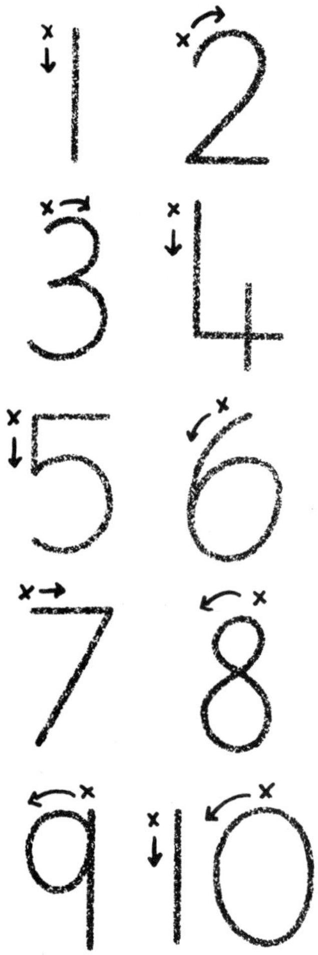

incidentally and informally during their time in school as well as through the formal lessons in this book. Similarly they will have been using number words and numerals as they have encountered them in their counting and other mathematical activities. During the course of these activities teachers will probably have demonstrated and taught the children how to write the numerals and, possibly, provided copy models of number words. The aim of these pages is to confirm and consolidate the teaching of correct formation of numerals and to provide models of correct spelling and letter formation of the number words one to ten. To give interest and meaning to the work and to enhance concept formation, the number words have been illustrated by an appropriate number of objects.

One is made starting at the top and moving downwards forms a vertical line.

Two begins at the top with a clockwise curve followed by a curved slope back to a point below the starting point. The figure concludes with a horizontal line from left to right. The numeral is made in one continuous movement without lifting the pencil from the paper.

Three starts with a clockwise curve which continues into a semi-circle followed by a similar but larger semi-circle below. The central turn is the emphatic element.

Four commences from the top with a vertical down-stroke continuing into a horizontal line from left to right. The cross-stroke is then added across the horizontal.

Five commences at the top with a vertical stroke leading into a clockwise curve. The horizontal line at the top is then added from left to right.

Six should be written with an anticlockwise direction. The loop is closed and should occupy approximately half the total height of the figure.

Seven is made in one continuous movement. The pencil makes a horizontal line from left to right. It then executes an angular turn and a diagonal line sloping backwards.

Eight should be written by starting at the top with an anticlockwise motion. This figure may need considerable practice.

Nine starts at the top with an anticlockwise motion. It should be written in one continuous movement.

In the case of number ten, one is drawn as previously illustrated and nought is the same as the letter *o*.

Teachers should demonstrate the figures to show children correct methods of formation. They should also advise the children that the numerals should all be written the same size.

During the lessons based on these pages, it will be helpful to read through the ten pairs of words and to encourage the children to count the objects that illustrate each number.

Page 32

'Simple Simon'

'Simple Simon' has been included to illustrate a number of teaching points. It is hoped that children will be familiar with the rhyme. The only capital letter involved is *S* which has the same shape as its lower-case equivalent.

The teacher should first read it to the children while they follow it in their books. Then the teacher should demonstrate writing the rhyme on the blackboard or other visual aid. As the teacher writes, opportunities arise to draw attention to the way writing should be set out. Guidance can be given on size of letters, spacing of letters, words and lines and the illustration of written work.

When the children write out the rhyme in their own writing books the teacher should circulate and give appropriate individual help. This will be an opportunity not only to observe the size and spacing of writing but also the accuracy, speed and rhythm of letter formation.

Although all teachers will be concerned to help the children improve the standard of their handwriting it must be emphasised that there should be no attempt to enforce conformity at this stage. There must be room for variations and the child's delight in writing is an important consideration.

Conclusion

It is assumed that, by the time they have worked through Pupils' Book A, most children will have made considerable progress in learning to write and that the standard of letter formation in their free writing will reflect, at least to some extent, the teaching provided in the formal lessons. However, individual pupils will still vary considerably in their abilities in many aspects of the skill. The following points will continue to be of concern to teachers in this respect:

Size of letters

Pupils should be given considerable freedom to make letters of a size appropriate to their degree of maturation and to set out and illustrate their work to their own satisfaction. They must, however, be given guidance on the size of writing appropriate to a given exercise and to the size of the writing sheet used.

It will be found that the majority of children in a class will all too readily tend to write as the teacher and classmates do, and to adopt the size of letters illustrated in the Pupils' Books and on cards made by the teacher. The teacher will mainly be concerned with children who have not developed sufficiently to be able to write letters as small as those illustrated in the

Pupils' Books, and with those who attempt to copy adults and much older children by writing far smaller letters than is desirable at this stage.

The letters illustrated in the Pupils' Books are of a size commonly written by the average pupil with pencil on paper at this stage, but as has already been emphasised, it would be wrong to expect all pupils in a class to write letters almost exactly of this size.

Spacing of letters and words

Guidance for the teacher on these aspects is given in Part 1, page 36. The space between words obviously depends on the size of the letters used. For letters of the size used in Pupils' Book A, the space between the words should be such that a finger can be placed between two words.

Distance between successive lines of writing

There is no hard and fast rule, but in general, it is better to have too much rather than too little space between lines of writing. There certainly should be no likelihood of descenders in one line touching ascenders in the next. The spacing of lines in the Pupils' Book gives a guide as to what might be expected at this stage.

Alignment and placement of exercise

Children should be taught to begin at the left-hand side of the page, to leave a space at the top of the page, to start a new line if there is insufficient room for the next word in the line, and, eventually, to leave margins at the side and bottom of the page. The majority of the children in a class will soon learn these lessons and will be helped by using the Pupils' Books, but there may be a few children in each class who will take longer to learn and will need continual help from the teacher until they overcome their difficulties.

A few children may have difficulty for some time in writing in a straight line across the page. Correction of faulty posture will generally quickly remedy this fault.

Speed and rhythm of writing

It has been continually emphasised that the development of fluent and rhythmical writing is of more importance at this stage than the acquisition of the ability to write near perfect letter forms. Although the children should continually strive to write better letter forms and the teacher must always encourage reasonably neat, tidy and careful work, it should be remembered that children will probably improve the standard of their letter forms as they mature, if they have learned to write freely and rhythmically at this stage.

Slow, cramped, over-careful writing laboriously performed in an attempt to acquire perfection of letter forms is not helpful.

Exercises such as those on pages 1–6 of Pupils' Book A should each be written several times. At the first attempt a passage may be written fairly slowly, but easily and rhythmically. It should be written several more times with care, but at gradually increasing speed on each occasion. Finally it can be written freely and easily in the children's exercise books and an appropriate illustration added.

Pupils' Book B

Contents

Book B covers the following:

- Rhythmic pattern exercises
- Revision of lower-case letters
- Systematic instruction and practice in making the 26 capital letters.
- Practice in using all letters in words arranged so that they serve as spelling lists as well as models for writing practice
- Instruction in alphabetical order
- Examples of continuous prose and poetry as models for sustained writing practice
- Word lists as a spelling resource for children's own writing.

List of contents

Further practice of these items will be found in the Infant Copymasters. Relevant copymasters for further practice are indicated in brackets. A full chart cross-referencing the Infant Copymasters to Pupils' Book B will be found on p. 141.

29 Word list: Food and Drink
30 Word list: Alphabetical Order
31 Poem: The Guppy
32 Comic Verse: I'm Not Frightened of Pussy Cats

Using Pupils' Book B

It is assumed that children will have worked through Pupils' Book A with some degree of success before being introduced to Pupils' Book B. At the same time as working through the exercises in Pupils' Book A children should have had many experiences to help them understand the purposes and conventions of writing. They will also have received some instruction in methods of writing capital letters even though these are not formally introduced in *New Nelson Handwriting* until Pupils' Book B.

At this stage in their development as writers the larger part of handwriting practice will arise through a variety of writing activities to be found in any good Infant class. Teachers will use the opportunities that naturally occur as children write stories, news, etc. to provide incidental advice and practice. However, this incidental teaching will rarely be sufficient and most children will benefit from regular formal instruction as outlined in *New Nelson Handwriting*.

While it is natural for teachers to seek high standards of work, and while each child may be expected to try to improve the quality of his/her writing, emphasis at this stage must continue to be on the freedom and fluency of writing rather than on laboured excellence of form. A child's success at a later stage will depend on the early establishment of sound writing techniques and an ability to write fluently and rhythmically. Although very speedy writing is not the aim at this stage, slow and laboured copying of patterns, exercises, letters and words should be discouraged.

Revision and remedial help

The first task of the teacher must be to assess the level of achievement of each child. The pupil's record, which may include an example of handwriting together with comments by the previous teacher, should help in this respect. The teacher should then be able to decide on the type and amount of revision necessary and how to group the children. It may be possible, at this stage, to do some revision and teaching of handwriting with the whole class.

When the children are busy writing in a practice period, the teacher should observe individual pupils, remembering that *how* the child writes is more important than the *look* of what is written.

The following points should be checked:

1. that the child is provided with a seat and table suited to his/her height and build.

2. that the child is seated correctly in a relaxed manner so that the hands and arms are able to move easily across the table.
3. that the child holds the pencil in a reasonably correct manner (see page 25).
4. that the child holds the pencil lightly.
5. that the child writes by movements of the hand and arm and not by flexing the fingers.
6. that the child writes fluently and rhythmically and not in a slow, laboured and jerky manner.
7. that the child writes individual letters as a unified movement starting in the correct place.
8. that left-handed pupils, in particular, have acquired satisfactory writing techniques.
9. that the child tries to do the following when writing:
   - start near the left-hand edge of the page
   - align writing across the page reasonably straight
   - leave appropriate spaces between letters, words and lines
   - write letters of a regular size
   - write a size suited to his/her degree of development
   - write letters of correct shapes and proportions
   - write pulled strokes vertical and parallel

Page by page guide

Pages 1–4

Rhythmic pattern exercises

The exercises illustrated on these four pages incorporate many of the movements used in the formation of letters. They should be performed over and over again until the child can reproduce them reasonably accurately and with easy, rhythmical movements. A variety of writing instruments including thick stemmed soft-lead pencils, coloured pencils, felt pens and ordinary HB lead pencils can be used. Children who find these exercises very difficult to perform can be taken back to the simpler exercises at the beginning of Pupils' Book A or to the scribbling exercises described in the preparatory section of this manual (see p. 62).

Page 1

Ovals

These exercises are designed to develop skill in making ovals. When demonstrating or supervising practice, teachers should emphasise ease and rhythm of production rather than accurate representation of the form. Children should be encouraged to make the ovals in a single, smooth and confident anticlockwise movement.

Page 2

Spirals, loops, swings and bridges

Clockwise and anticlockwise movements are required in these exercises. The need for careful perception and controlled fluent movement in order to reproduce the range of patterns illustrated provides good training for handwriting. The manner in which lines of pattern interact to form combined patterns provides teachers with an opportunity to emphasise uniformity of shape and size. If the elements of each pattern are not reasonably uniform the effect of the combined patterns will be lost.

Pages 3 and 4

Straight line exercises and patterns

These exercises demand precision of movement and give practice in making most of the lines involved in forming capital letters. Although at first they may be performed relatively slowly, the aim should be to provide sufficient practice for children to be able to produce them through confident, fluent and accurate movements.

All of the patterns illustrated on pages 1–4 can be repeated by children as decoration for their written work at any stage. A well-formed and coloured strip of pattern provides a most pleasing decoration for a piece of well-presented work.

Page 5

Revision: *a, c, d, g, o, g; i, j, k, l, t*

Practice is provided in writing these letters both individually and as words. Attention is drawn to the uniform size of letters together with the correct proportions of ascenders and descenders through the use of triple lines.

Children who experience difficulty in maintaining reasonable letter proportions may be helped by the provision of specially lined paper for some of their work.

All children will benefit from:

1. Preliminary rhythm exercises: anticlockwise, continuous ovals and spirals; swings pattern.
2. Having the correct method of constructing each letter in a group briefly revised and demonstrated. Pupils with severe difficulty in making these letters need to return to practise Pupils' Book A pages 7–10 and 15–19.
3. Sufficient practice based on the models on page 5 to enable them to write the letters and words speedily, rhythmically and correctly.

Page 6

Revision: *e, f, s, u; b, p*

The page plan and teaching procedures are the same as for page 5. Less able pupils requiring additional revision should be referred back to Pupils' Book A pages 12–14, 20 and 21.

Page 7

Revision: *h, m, n, r, v, w, x, y, z*

The page plan and teaching procedures are the same as for page 5. Less able pupils requiring additional revision should be referred back to Pupils' Book A pages 20–24, and 26–29.

Pages 8–12

Capital letters

Five pages are devoted to the systematic teaching of the 26 capital letters. For convenience, they have been divided into five groups according to the method of construction. The same general page plan has been followed for all five pages.

At the top and bottom of each page is a row of pattern incorporating some of the movements used in writing the particular group of capital letters. After the teacher has demonstrated the pattern, the children should practise it several times to develop fluency and to relax their muscles ready for the learning task which follows.

It is assumed that teachers will go over the page with their pupils and explain that, in each case, the lower-case version of the letter is followed by one or more examples of the capital letter as models for practice and to illustrate relative heights. There are two proper nouns for each letter so that the children can practise writing words involving capital letters. The words should, of course, be read to the children so that they they know what they are writing. The first proper noun in each case is a first name. Care has been taken to choose names that reflect some of the many different cultural groups to be found in British schools. The second noun is the name of a place and it is expected that teachers will discuss these at a level appropriate to the children's general knowledge.

When children are learning to form capital letters correctly they will need to practise each one many times. They might write at least a full line of each, based on the model in the Pupils' Book. Similarly, all the words should be practised many times. Additionally, children could be asked to think of other names beginning with the same letter.

Ideally, capital letters should be the same height as letters with ascenders i.e. slightly less than twice the 'x' height. However, at this age, most children are better advised to make capitals twice the height of lower-case letters without ascenders. Advice on this and the varying widths of capital letters is to be found in Chapter 8 of Part 1 of this manual.

Page 8

Straight stroke, one movement capitals: *I, J, L, V, W,* and *Z*

Apart from the curved foot of the capital letter *J*, these six capitals are all made from straight lines. In each case the starting point is at the top and, except in the case of *Z*, the first movement is downwards. In the case of *Z* the first movement is from left to right. Arrows have been drawn alongside the models in the Pupils' Book to indicate starting point and direction of movement but it is also important to emphasise that these letters should be made in one continuous movement without lifting the pencil from the paper.

Considerable practice may be needed before children can write these capitals speedily, confidently and accurately, and many children are helped by rhythmically talking through the movement e.g. for letter *V*: 'come down diagonally to the writing line and back up again to the top.'

Page 9

Rounded, one movement capitals: *C, G, O, S* and *U*

With the exception of *U*, these capital letters start at one o'clock. They are all made with one continuous, anticlockwise, and curved movement. It should be pointed out that the capital *C*, *O* and *S* are the same shape, though roughly twice as tall, as their lower-case counterparts. The changed shape of capital *G* will require extra attention and the absence of a cross-bar should be emphasised. Similarly, emphasis should be given to the way the capital *U* ends at the top of the letter. There is no final downstroke as there is with a lower-case *u*.

Children will need considerable practice in making these five capital letters, and in making the related patterns, before they can be expected to write them confidently and well at a reasonable speed.

Page 10

Straight stroke, two movement capitals: *M, N, T, X* and *Y*

These capital letters are made entirely from straight lines and each one requires two separate pencil movements. Care must be taken to ensure that the second line relates accurately to the first.

In each case the first line starts at the top and moves downwards, though in the case of *X* and *Y* the direction is diagonal. There are several possible methods of constructing these letters but the recommended manner is illustrated in Chapter 8 of Part 1 of this manual and in the Pupils' Book. Numbered arrows have been used to indicate which line to make first, where to start and which direction to move towards.

When demonstrating, teachers should emphasise the following:

1. The last three lines of *M* and the last two of *N* are made without lifting the pencil.
2. The cross-bar of *T* is added last.

The diagonals of *X* must cross in the middle.

4. The first diagonal of *Y* is a half line and meets the second diagonal at its centre.

Again, considerable practice will be needed.

Page 11

Rounded, two movement capitals: *B, D, P, Q* and *R*

These capital letters involve both curved and straight lines. Except in the case of *Q*, the straight vertical lines should always be made first, starting at the top and moving down. In the case of *Q*, the anticlockwise oval is made first and then the cross-stroke added. The curved parts of *B*, *D*, *P* and *R* are made in a continuous clockwise movement without lifting the pencil.

The correct method of making these letters and the recommended proportions are illustrated in Chapter 8 of Part 1 of this teacher's manual and in the Pupils' Book. The curved part of letters *B*, *D*, *P* and *R* should commence at the top of the vertical line. However, when writing quickly it may be difficult to ensure that the curve starts exactly at the top of the line. In that case it is better for the curve to overhang slightly than to stop short of the vertical.

In the case of *B*, *P* and *R* the point of intersection with the vertical line should be approximately half-way down.

Once again, considerable practice will be required before the children will have the confidence to write these capitals fluently, quickly and well.

Page 12

Straight stroke, three movement capitals: *A, E, F, H* and *K*

Each of these five capitals is made with three straight line movements. In each case the first line starts at the top and comes down. In the case of *E* this first vertical line then continues horizontally. The cross-bar of *A*, *E*, *F* and *H* occurs at approximately halfway down the letter as does the meeting point of the two diagonals of letter *K*.

The correct method of writing these capitals is described and illustrated in Chapter 8 of Part 1 of this manual and in the Pupils' Book. Three arrows have been added to the illustrations to show recommended sequence, direction and starting point of the lines. As described in Chapter 8, the capital *A* seems better balanced when the cross-bar is slightly lower than mid-height.

Ample practice will be needed for children to become quick and confident in writing these capitals well.

Page 13

Writing revision, spelling and vocabulary lists

This is one of fourteen such pages. See page 95 for detailed notes on this page.

Pages 14 and 15

The Alphabet

On these pages the 26 letters of the alphabet are introduced in alphabetical order. For each letter there is an illustration of an easily recognised object beginning with the letter concerned. A model of both the lower-case and capital form of the letter then follows. These pages provide a checklist of correct letter shapes to which children should be encouraged to refer when in doubt.

Teachers will also wish to use these pages as an opportunity to teach alphabetical order and to encourage children to commit the sequence to memory. A wall frieze of the letters in alphabetical order is useful at this stage to consolidate learning.

Pages 16, 17, 31 and 32

Continuous prose and poetry

These four pages provide examples of continuous prose and poetry so that the children can gain experience of writing in a sustained and continuous manner. While demonstrating to the children, and again while they are actually practising, opportunities will arise to reinforce good writing habits.

Now is also the time to focus their attention on other more detailed writing features, such as appropriate spacing for letters, words and lines. If necessary, children should be encouraged to write the pieces out several times until they achieve satisfactory standards of presentation.

The pieces have been carefully selected both for length and interest. Teachers will be concerned that their pupils know the Green Cross Code and its inclusion as a writing model should provide the opportunity to reinforce other teaching about road safety. The poem and limerick have been included for the children's enjoyment. Indeed it is hoped that they will lead to the requests for further examples of poetry of this kind.

Pages 16 and 17

The Green Cross Code

This has been arranged to fit a double page. First it should be read aloud by the teacher and then again, perhaps by the more able readers. In the course of the discussion which will inevitably follow, the teacher can explain or reinforce points as necessary. Many children will have incidents and anecdotes they will want to contribute and interest should be high.

Before the children commence writing the teacher may want to demonstrate good practice or remind the children of rules to remember. Finally the children might paint pictures or make models on this theme. The code is surely of sufficient importance to be worth committing to memory which would be a contribution to memory training as well as to road safety.

Page 31

'The Guppy'

This poem should first be read to the class several times and unfamiliar vocabulary explained, if possible with the help of illustrations. Before the children are asked to write it out the teacher should write it on the blackboard to demonstrate good practice and to emphasise the special rules for writing out poetry: that each line of poetry must start on a new line and commence with a capital letter. The rhyming pattern might also be discussed.

Further development might include illustrating the poem, finding other Ogden Nash verse to enjoy and committing a favourite example to memory.

Page 32

'I'm Not Frightened Of Pussy Cats'

This poem should be read two or three times for enjoyment before the children are asked to write it out. The humour, rhyme and rhythm of the poem should be discussed. It is worth reminding children of the conventions of writing out poetry. While the children are writing, the teacher should observe carefully, and intervene as necessary.

Follow-up work might include illustrating the poem or finding and reading further examples of Spike Milligan's work. It is quite likely that some children will already know a few limericks. With a little prompting, children might be encouraged to make up some of their own.

Page 13 and pages 18–30

Writing revision, spelling and vocabulary lists

These fourteen pages are designed to achieve several aims at once, and it is important that teachers appreciate their various functions so that children obtain the maximum benefit. The lists are intended to serve as:

1. Models for handwriting practice
   All letters of the alphabet, lower-case and capital, are included as they occur naturally in the words.
2. Collections of related words for vocabulary development
   It will, therefore, be necessary to read through the words and discuss their meanings with the children.
3. A spelling source for children's free writing
   If children are to be as independent as possible in their use of these spelling lists they must be made familiar with the content and order of the pages involved.

Time spent on training children in efficient use of the word lists will be time well spent. It will also be helpful to draw attention to specific pages which relate to topics of current interest.

The words provided on these fourteen pages are classified under clear headings. They have been selected because they are likely to be used frequently by children of this age and stage of development.

When children are using the lists as a basis for handwriting practice, it will continue to be necessary to observe the writing process as well as evaluating the end product. Any faults noticed should be attended to immediately and, if necessary, children should be referred back to the relevant pages in Pupils' Books A or B so that they can overcome the problem.

The fourteen headings covered in this way are as follows

Pages 31 and 32

Refer back to page 94 of this manual for advice on teaching these pages.

Teaching the joined style

Introducing joined writing

A school's policy for handwriting will normally recommend when pupils should be introduced to joined writing. However, it is impossible to prescribe an age at which *all* children should be taught to do joined writing as such a decision must depend on:

a) the ability of the children.

b) their previous experience of writing.

c) the views of the teachers involved.

The age of seven or eight years seems to be generally favoured for the change to be introduced, and this seems particularly suitable, when, as in the case of the Nelson style, the joined style is a natural progression from the fluent print script which precedes it.

In Britain many children transfer from Infant to Junior classes at seven years plus and, as the vast majority of pupils change teachers on the September following their seventh birthday, it would seem unwise to launch into a major development in handwriting style before pupils have fully adjusted to their new class. For this reason the introduction of joined writing is often left until the Spring term of the first year of what is traditionally the Junior Stage. This allows time for teachers to get to know their pupils, to gauge their strengths and weaknesses and, particularly, to observe their writing habits. Pages 1 and 2 of Pupils' Book 1 are designed to help teachers and children ensure good habits of posture and pencil grip as well as correct letter formation. During the Autumn term there will be ample opportunity to observe children as they write in the normal course of classroom activities as well as in periods specifically set aside for handwriting practice. Those children whose performance is unsatisfactory should be given individual attention and may be taken back to appropriate pages in Pupils' Books A and B, and given additional practice with relevant exercises from the Infant Copymasters. Thus, by judicious encouragement and remedial teaching, the majority of pupils should be ready to begin learning Nelson joined writing by the Spring term.

The teacher is reminded that the two essential prerequisites for success with the Nelson joined style are as follows:

a) the ability to produce the recommended writing patterns fluently and well so that the elements of each pattern are consistent in height and width

b) the ability to write each letter in the Infant Writing rhythmically, speedily and well so that, when writing expressively, little conscious attention need be paid to individual letter forms or to the writing process.

The writing process

Teachers' attitudes to the whole process of writing are of great importance throughout their use of *New Nelson Handwriting*. Pupils need to be aware that the attainment of a pleasant, legible hand is necessary. However, they also need to understand that it is but one of the secretarial skills used for effective communication in writing. They must also come to accept that, while painstakingly beautiful handwriting may be desirable for final versions of publishing writing, there are other occasions when speed is important and when writing which is legible and reasonably neat is adequate.

The approach to teaching writing in many primary and middle schools is moving in a direction which might well be labelled the 'Graves approach', since Donald Graves' book *Writing: Teachers and Children at Work* has been a highly influential factor. The essentials of the approach discussed in this book may be summarised as a partnership in the craft of writing in which teachers function as models, counsellors and supporters while pupils develop and practise the skills and arts of written composition for their own understood purposes.

Graves analyses the writing process into several key headings:

1. Rehearsal. This is the stage of preparation for composition. It can take the form of daydreaming, sketching, brainstorming lists of ideas and/or words, outlining, reading, researching or discussing, in order to collect and/or clarify ideas.
2. Drafting. The writing of the first attempt at expressing these ideas. At this stage, handwriting need be no more than barely legible. It should, moreover, be fast enough to keep pace with the flow of ideas and language. At this stage there is no need for undue concern about accuracy in spelling - this could be a time for invented spellings!
3. Revising. The writer now reviews what (s)he has written. Alterations will be made to the text to clarify or enrich meaning. Words may be substituted or deleted, word order may be changed, and sentences and even paragraphs may be rearranged.
4. Editing. This is the time to pay attention to the secretarial skills of spelling, punctuation, grammar etc. Children often need advice at this point and teachers intervene as appropriate to the pupils' level of development.
5. Publishing. This final stage is the occasion for best calligraphy as, freed from other concerns, the pupil is able to concentrate on penmanship.

Children do not necessarily have to go through all five stages every time they write. Some notes and messages and many routine classroom exercises need be written only once. On the other hand, stories, poems, plays, diaries, topic reports and other creative, purposeful writing experiences may be enhanced through the use of some or all of the strategies listed. Teachers following the 'Graves approach' do not require their pupils to bring every piece of creative writing to a polished finish for publishing. Indeed, 20% is a proportion often quoted, the other 80% of pieces remaining in the pupils' exercise books as revised and/or edited drafts.

At the time of writing, many teachers will also be considering the implications for their work of *The Report of the Committee of Inquiry into the Teaching of English Language*. This report, commonly known as 'the Kingman report', recognises the trend in writing described above and suggests that the individual, group and class conferences which are encouraged at all stages in the writing process provide excellent opportunities for teaching *about* language and the ways in which meaning is made.

On page 33 of the report the following point is made:

'For the discussion of the first draft to be helpful, teacher and pupil need to be able to use a shared vocabulary for talking about writing. There is much more to writing than spelling and punctuation. Is it clear, in general, what the writer is writing about - is "the topic" clearly identified? Is it clear who the participants are - is "the referent" in each case clearly identified? Would it be clearer to use a richer "adjective" or a different "noun"? Is there a "sentence" which seems too long - what makes it too long and how might the problem be remedied? Is there "a paragraph" which is too long - what makes it too long and what makes you decide to break a paragraph in one place rather than another? Is there an expression which jars, which does not seem to fit in very well - is there "a synonym" which would suit this type of writing better?'

This quotation from the Kingman report has been included because, together with the theoretical discussions above, it emphasises the complexity of the writing process and the sensitivity of the teacher's role. These issues were very much in mind when the *New Nelson Handwriting* materials were developed. They aim to cater for the mechanical skills of cursive handwriting within the broad context of the writer's craft.

The joined writing course

Pupils' Books 1–4 provide a complete course in joined writing from the introduction of the Nelson joined style to the development of an individual style.

Teachers are reminded of the importance of discussing each page with the pupils, of demonstrating the techniques involved and then of observing the children while they practise. Each exercise should be performed several times, if necessary, until pupils can write the particular elements quickly and well. Further variety and practice is provided by appropriate exercises in the Junior Copymasters.

Before children commence the course of lessons on Nelson joined writing teachers should explain that there are several rules to be learned and practised before the style can be written satisfactorily. It is most important that while they are learning these rules, all other written work is done in unjoined print.

At intervals throughout the four Pupils' Books the children are encouraged to assess their own progress and to check their written work for mistakes. It is expected that teachers will draw attention to this aspect of the work as it is introduced in the Pupils' Books but that they will also initiate additional self-evaluation exercises as necessary.

The notes for teachers which follow this section are less full than those provided for Pupils' Books A and B. This is because instructions to pupils are included on many pages in Pupils' Books 1–4 and these will also serve as reminders for teachers. In Pupils' Books 2–4 where practice in handwriting has been closely allied to learning in other subjects, advice for the teacher will be given where appropriate.

Pupils' Book 1

Contents

Pupils' Book 1 covers the following:

- Revision of correct posture and pencil grip, pattern making to revise good techniques
- Revision of print letters and numerals
- Systematic teaching of the joined style through five rules for joining
- Ample practice of the joined style
- Introduction to the idea of self-assessment
- Introduction of speed tests

List of contents

Further practice of these items will be found in the Junior Copymasters. Relevant copymasters for further practice are indicated in brackets. A full chart cross-referencing the Junior Copymasters to Pupils' Book 1 will be found on p. 142.

Page by page guide

Page 1

Revision of correct posture and pencil grip; pattern making to revise good techniques

Ensure that children are provided with suitable chairs and tables. Discuss the pictures on page 1 and refer back to them through the year as necessary. Encourage the children to establish a habit of regularly checking their own posture and pencil grip.

As the children perform the pattern exercises illustrated, observe them carefully for good posture and pencil hold but also for relaxed, light and rhythmical movements. The children will benefit from several sessions of this pattern making to consolidate good writing habits.

It is important that the children should understand that they must continue to use their unjoined print script for all other writing while they are working through Pupils' Book 1 and learning the basic rules of the joined style.

Page 2

Revision of print letters (lower-case and capitals) and numerals

This page is included so that teachers can make sure that letters and numerals are being formed correctly and fluently. Attention should be drawn to the connection between families of lower-case letters and the related pattern.

Teachers are reminded that children are not expected to make exact and immaculate reproductions of the prototype letter forms illustrated in the Pupils' Book. Children must have a clear conception of these letter forms but, while their efforts must of course be instantly recognisable, they will probably have a certain liveliness and character which the more precise models in the Pupils' Book lack. On no account should children be allowed to write slowly and meticulously in order to obtain exact reproductions of the prototypes. Junior Copymaster 7 will be found useful at this point.

Page 3

Introduction to the joined style

In accordance with accepted good teaching practice the children are introduced to an example of the full Nelson joined handwriting style which they are about to learn. They should be cautioned against attempting to reproduce the style before they have learnt its elements.

The sentence beginning 'At exactly six o'clock' was devised to include all 26 lower-case letters, and children should be encouraged to compare the cursive version with the one produced in print script. The teacher is advised to guide the pupils in a letter by letter comparison, pointing out the addition of hooks and noting those letters which change significantly.

It is assumed that the teacher will read the extract to the children and discuss it with them as it is always essential to ensure that the content of a piece of writing is understood.

Page 4

Changes to *f*, *k*, *r* and *y*

Special attention is now paid to f, *k*, *r* and *y*, the four letters which change significantly from the Nelson print script to the Nelson joined style. It is recommended that the notes for the pupils are first discussed with them. The children should then practise these letter changes by tracing over the large model letters and by reproducing the lines of normal sized models.

Page 5

Lower-case letters with hooks

This page provides a further opportunity to study and practise the form of all 26 lower-case letters used in Nelson joined handwriting. The instructions on the pupils' page should be discussed with the pupils and they should be encouraged to practise making the letters until they can make them correctly in one smooth, continuous movement. (The letters *f*, *t*, *x*, *i* and j, of course, require an additional movement to make the cross-stroke or dot.)

Children should now use these revised letter forms whenever they write lower-case letters in isolation. Junior Copymaster 8 will be found useful at this point.

Page 6

Ascenders and descenders

Dotted guidelines have been added here to draw attention to the relative heights and proportion of letters particularly those with ascenders and descenders. Teachers should ensure that these two technical terms are understood by the children. Capital letters are also revised and their relative heights emphasised.

Particular attention should be paid to the size of the letters and the correct alignment of ascenders and descenders when children practise this page.

Page 7

The basic join: joining Set 1 to Set 2 letters

The children are introduced to the first element of the joined style, the *basic join*. The notes in the Pupils' Book describe the connection between the upstroke of the swings pattern and the way joins are made. Just as the swings pattern should always be made rhythmically and fluently so should the basic join. It is also important for children to become aware of the way in which the basic join is made from the hook at the end of one letter to the starting point of the next.

To clarify the different types of join, letters have been divided into five sets (see Ready Reference p. 3). It is assumed that children of this age will already be familiar with the principle of forming sets according to given criteria.

Pages 8–11

Practising the basic join:

On these four pages further attention is paid to the basic join. Various combinations of Set 1 and Set 2 letters are set out as models for practice. As children trace over the large model prototypes or reproduce the lines of examples, the teacher should observe them carefully to ensure that letters and joins are made rhythmically and correctly, and that the pencil is not lifted from the paper between letters.

Pages 12

Joining from Set 1 letters to *e*

Attention is drawn to the shape of the letter *e* in cursive writing when it follows a letter with a hook. Teachers should explain that the 45° upstroke from the base of the Set 1 letter serves not only to join the two letters but also to form the diagonal part of the letter *e*.

Examples of this join are provided as models for practice. In the words at the foot of the page letters are not joined unless the join involved is the basic join. The other form of the letter *e* is dealt with on page 21.

Page 13

Joining from Set 1 letters to *s*

Attention is now drawn to the form of the letter *s* in cursive writing when it follows a letter with a hook. Teachers should explain that the join made by the stroke coming up from the base of the Set 1 letter gives the *s* its pointed top. It would be unnatural and unnecessary to give the *s* a rounded top here.

Examples of this join are provided as models for practice. In the words at the foot of the page letters are not joined unless the join involved is the basic one. Another form of letter *s* is dealt with on page 22.

Page 14

The basic join revised

Eight letters belong to Sets 1 and 2. A Venn diagram showing the intersection of Sets 1 and 2 will illustrate clearly that *i*, *a*, *c*, *d*, *e*, *m*, *n* and *u* are members of both sets:

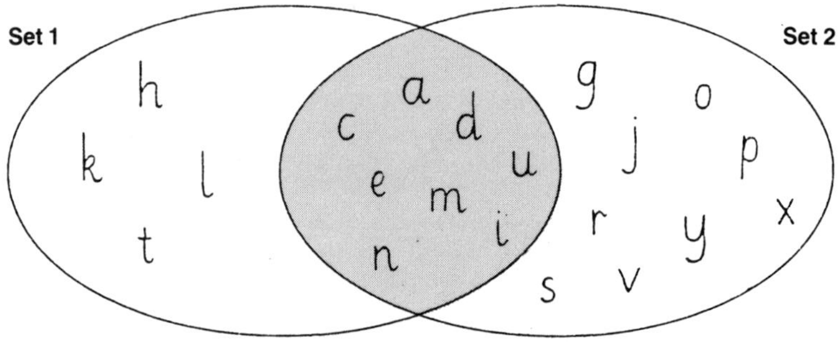

Venn diagram to illustrate the intersection of Sets 1 and 2.

Teachers should explain that, because these letters all have identical hooks and entry points, they can be joined together in any sequence by using the basic join. The children should then be encouraged to write varying strings of the 8 letters by using the basic join. The children should be encouraged to write the strings continuously and fluently. After writing they should check for mistakes.

Examples of words containing only those 8 letters are also provided as models for practice. Children should be encouraged to think of some more words that can be written with these 8 letters.

Attention is again drawn to the relative heights of ascenders and descenders and to the importance of practising the swings pattern.

Page 15

The second join

The second join is now taught. Letters with ascenders on their left side are classified as Set 3: *b*, *f*, *h*, *k*, *l* and *t*. When these letters follow Set 1 letters the second join is used. A large model of the join is provided for observation, discussion and tracing. Teachers should also demonstrate the join emphasising that it is essentially the same up-stroke of the swings pattern that was used for the basic join. However, it is important for the children to understand that the second join is effected approximately halfway up the ascender. The pencil then travels up to the top of the letter and down again to the base in one continuous movement.

Examples of pairs of letters linked by the second join are provided for practice. Teachers should observe pupils at practice and watch for significant faults. Two faults which often occur when joins are made from Set 1 to Set 3 letters are:

1. Effecting the join at, or near the base of, the letter with the ascender. This gives rise to cramped writing with letters too close together.

2. Taking the up-stroke up to the top of the ascender. This results either in letters being too far apart or the angle of join being halved to 22½°.

The following points are among the accepted criteria for judging writing:

a) all letters in a word should be equidistant

b) all joins should be at a constant angle (i.e. all joining strokes should be parallel)

It is very important, therefore, for children to be able to make this join correctly. Children will vary considerably in the amount of practice they will require in order to make this join satisfactorily.

Page 16 and 17

Practising the second join

Additional examples of the second join are provided as models for practice. Extra emphasis is placed on the joins to letters *f* and *t* as these may prove difficult.

Page 18

Checks on writing habits; pattern making

This page of pattern practice is provided to encourage children to experiment with various combinations of pattern elements. At the same time the habit of self-assessment is encouraged. Teachers too should check that the pupils are sitting properly and that they make the patterns rhythmically and fluently. Some children may need repeated practice to achieve the desired effect but the exercises should be relaxing and enjoyable. Regularity and consistency of size and form is encouraged by the realisation that the patterns do not work unless they are uniform. Children will also enjoy colouring in the patterns and may use bands of similar patterns to decorate other work.

Page 19

The third join: joining Set 4 to Set 2 letters

The third join is the one which links letters of Set 4 (*f*, *o*, *r*, *v* and *w*) with those of Set 2. A large model of the join is provided for observation, discussion and tracing. Teachers should also demonstrate the join emphasising that it is a shallow horizontal curve. The children should also understand that the distance between the two joined letters should be the same as that between letters when joined by the basic or by the second join. Some examples of the join are also provided as models for practice.

Page 20

Practising the third join

More examples of the third join are provided as models for practice.

Page 21

Joining Set 4 letters to *e*

Attention is drawn to the form of the letter *e* when it follows a Set 4 letter. Large models of the join are provided for observation, discussion and tracing. However, teachers should also demonstrate the join emphasising the special shape of the bowl of the letter *e* resulting from the shallow horizontal curved join.

Examples of the join are provided as models for practice and the page concludes with further suggestions for practice.

Page 22

Joining Set 4 letters to *s*

Attention is drawn to the form of letter *s* when it follows a Set 4 letter. Large models of the join are provided for observation, discussion and tracing. Teachers should demonstrate the join and emphasise that the flattened top of the *s* results from the horizontal joining stroke.

Examples of the join are provided as models for practice, and the page concludes with more patterns for practice.

Page 23

The fourth join

The fourth join is the one which joins letters of Set 4 to letters of Set 3. Large models of the join are provided for observation, discussion and tracing. Teachers should also demonstrate the join. It should be noted that the fourth join is really the same as the basic join except that it is made from the top of ordinary letters to the top of ascenders. In practice it is likely that this join will be made somewhere towards the top of the ascender rather than at the very top and this tendency is quite acceptable.

Examples of the join are provided as models for practice together with further revision of the swings pattern to emphasise the connection between the fourth join and the up-stroke of the swings pattern.

Page 24

Practising the fourth join

More examples of the fourth join are provided for additional practice.

A large model of the join for double *f* is included for observation, discussion and tracing. The teacher should also demonstrate this join to ensure that pupils understand that the bar of the first *f* joins directly to the top of the second *f* and that the second bar is added last of all.

Models of double *f* are provided, and it is probable that some children will need a considerable amount of practice before they can write double *f* confidently and well.

Page 25

The break letters: *b*, *g*, *j*, *p*, *q*, *s*, *x*, *y*, and *z*

Joins are never made after these nine letters. The reasons for not joining after the break letters are as follows:

- *g*, *j*, *p*, *q*, and *y* are not joined to the letter which follows because each of these letters concludes with a descender and any attempt to join from the base of a descender to the correct point on the next letter would result in either doubling the distance between the letters or halving the angle of the ligature stroke.
- *b* and *s* are not joined to the letter which follows because both these letters conclude with a curve made in a direction opposite to the flow of the writing and any attempt to effect a join would be unnatural and, possibly, ugly.
- *x* and *z* are not joined to the letter which follows because both of these letters are comprised of straight lines only and any attempt to make a join by adding a hook would fundamentally alter the shape of the letter.

Examples of words which include break letters are provided as models for practice. All joins learned will also be practised in the process.

Page 26

Revision of all joins

The swings pattern and all five categories of join are revised and practised on this page. Any children experiencing difficulty in effecting any joining movement should be taken back to the appropriate page for remedial attention.

The sentence beginning 'A quick brown fox' gives the children an opportunity to concentrate on their writing speed. However, teachers should explain to children that they should only attempt to increase their writing speed gradually, without sacrificing accuracy, rhythm or fluency.

Page 27

Capital letters and joined writing

These particular patterns and the list of proper names are included as models for practising capital letters. As the capitals in Nelson joined writing are the same as in Pupils' Books A and B the children should have little difficulty in this revision work. Teachers should stress that capital letters are never joined to lower-case letters.

The names should be read through and discussed as appropriate. For example, the terms 'first' name, 'Christian' name and 'given' name could give rise to interesting discussion. Care has been taken to include some names that reflect the many different cultural groups to be found in British schools. Teachers may also wish to take the opportunity to discuss alphabetical order. Only 24 names are listed in this alphabetical list because of shortage of space. The letters *x* and *z* were not included because relatively few first names commence with either of those letters.

When the pupils practise writing the names they should take care over the joined part of each word as well as over capital letters. As a follow-up exercise, the pupils could be instructed to think up and write out another list of names in alphabetical order.

Page 28

Revision of numbers

The aim of this page is to provide revision in the correct formation of figures. The instructions in the Pupils' Book are comprehensive but teachers may wish to demonstrate and discuss the points made in the notes.

Page 29

Practice of all joins; Spot the connection

The words on this page contain all the letters and types of join as they occur randomly.

Children should write out each group of words carefully, puzzle out what links the members of the group together and explain the connection in writing. It may be necessary for the teacher to read through the words and to discuss their meaning with the children.

The connections are as follows:

Group 1	All five words mean *big*.
Group 2	All five words are parts of a car.
Group 3	All five words are verbs.
Group 4	All four words are palindromes (words which read the same backwards).
Group 5	All four words are adjectives.
Group 6	All four words contain double consonants.

Pages 30–32

Poems as models for practice: 'Solomon Grundy', 'The old owl', 'Autumn'

The final three pages of Pupils' Book 1 contain poems as models for sustained practice in writing the full Nelson joined style. The children should be reminded of all the rules they have learned and required to check their work. The poems should, of course, be read aloud and discussed before the children write them. They have been selected in the hope that they will be enjoyed.

On page 31 special attention is paid to ascenders and descenders while on page 32 the children are again encouraged to increase their speed of writing without sacrificing accuracy, rhythm or fluency.

Conclusion

During the time taken to work through Pupils' Book 1 and to learn and practise all elements of the Nelson joined writing style, pupils should have continued to use Nelson Infant Writing for all other writing. If children have successfully completed the exercises in Pupils' Book 1, and satisfactorily reproduced the poems at the end of the book, they should be ready to use the joined style for all written work. It is important to encourage pupils to persist in using the joined style for all their written work. If they are allowed to vacillate they may fail to become committed to the joined style and they may not develop successfully an individual, fast-flowing style.

Pupils' Book 2

Contents

Pupils' Book 2 covers the following:

- Revision of correct posture and pencil grip
- Pattern making to revise good writing techniques
- Revision of the lower-case alphabet in the form required for Nelson joined writing
- Revision of capital letters and numerals
- Revision of the four types of join and the break letters
- Prose, poetry and limericks as models for practice
- Exercises in self-assessment
- Speed tests
- An emphasis on writing and spelling

List of contents

Further practice at the Pupils' Book 2 level will be found in the Junior Copymasters. Copymasters 18–22 provide sustained writing practice at the Book 2 level and emphasise an awareness of self-assessment when writing.

Page by page guide

Page 1

Revision of correct posture and pencil grip; pattern making to revise good writing techniques

Ensure that children are provided with suitable chairs and tables. Discuss the pictures on page one of the Pupils' Book and refer back to them throughout the year as necessary. Encourage children to continue the practice of regularly checking their own posture and pencil grip.

Although all pupils should now be writing joined Nelson handwriting for all their written work they will still benefit from frequent revision exercises and reminders to write lightly and smoothly. As children practise the pattern exercises illustrated on this page teachers should observe them carefully and intervene as necessary.

Children should, of course, be encouraged to reproduce the patterns accurately but rhythm and reasonable speed should not be sacrificed in the pursuit of a rigid uniformity.

Page 2

Revision of the lower-case alphabet in the form required for Nelson joined writing. Revision of capital letters and numerals

By now pupils should be thoroughly conversant with the forms of all the letters used in Nelson joined writing. However, it is so important that pupils are able to write them confidently, smoothly and quickly that some time must be set aside for further practice. Teachers should pay particular attention to the shapes of the rounded parts of letters and ensure that these are oval. They should also check that the letters *a, d, h, i, k, l, m, n, r, t* and *u* are all given hooks. Capital letters and numerals are also included for revision practice.

The models of the lower-case letters in the Pupils' Books are arranged in alphabetical order but additional practice can be provided by grouping them according to the method of their formation and to the associated pattern:

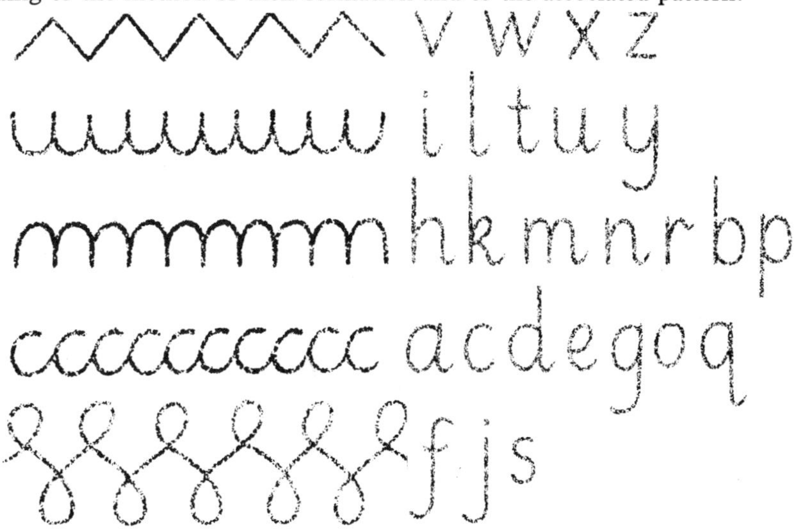

Page 3 and 4

Revision of all joins and the break letters

Teachers should work through both pages with the children and emphasise the correct way of making each join by demonstrating it on the blackboard. Each of the large models should then be used as the basis for practice.

The lists of words should be read through before the children practise the joins they contain. When the children have completed this writing task they should examine their work critically and rewrite any word with which they are dissatisfied.

During these exercises teachers should observe the children as they write and be ready to intervene in cases of serious difficulty. Then, when the pupils hand in the completed exercises, their writing should be checked again and significant errors pointed out to them. If fundamental faults are occurring it may be necessary to take a child back to the relevant pages of Pupils' Book 1 or the Junior Copymasters.

Pages 5–8

Prose, limericks and poems as models for practice

These four pages provide sustained practice in continuous writing of the Nelson joined style. All aspects of the children's knowledge of the writing process are called into play.

Each of the passages should be read aloud for pleasure and then used as a basis for class discussion. One of the author's major considerations when selecting material for writing practice was that the content of the passages chosen should serve a number of educational purposes, including vocabulary building. Teachers should ensure that they explain any unfamiliar words to the children carefully so that they may extend their vocabulary as a result.

Again many opportunities will arise for incidental teaching. On page 5, for instance, attention could be drawn to the collective noun for a group of lions as well as to the proper nouns for the female, male and young of the species. Also on page 5, a small amount of factual knowledge is given and the children might be set the task of finding out more about lions.

The limericks and poems on pages 6–8 provide opportunities to discuss rhyme and rhythm. Some children might be encouraged to learn one or more of these and to recite them to the class. The poem by Christina Rossetti could serve as an introduction to a project on precious stones.

Page 9

Direction of strokes

The purpose of this exercise is to make children aware of another criterion for judging the quality of their writing i.e. that down-strokes should all be parallel and diagonal joins consistently angled at approximately 45°. Teachers should go through the page with their pupils discussing the points thoroughly and demonstrating good practice on the blackboard. Explanation in the Pupils' Book has been made as full as possible as it is intended that children should refer back to this page from time to time.

Page 10

An exercise in self-assessment

This page is intended to encourage children to make a habit of evaluating their own progress as writers. They are asked to write Ogden Nash's poem 'The Rhinoceros' carefully and well. They are then asked to examine what they have written in accordance with the eight criteria which are listed on this page. Next they are expected to rewrite the poem carefully correcting any faults made in their first attempt. Finally, they are asked to write it out again without any mistakes but this time more quickly.

Teachers should go through the page with the children and read the poem to them. The adjective *homely* should be discussed with the children as most will probably be unaware that it means *plain and unattractive in appearance*. While the children work through this exercise teachers should observe them carefully, intervening as appropriate and generally encouraging a helpful attitude to self-assessment.

Page 11

Writing quickly and well

'A Tickle Rhyme' should first be read aloud; it is a light-hearted piece intended for the children's amusement. Teachers should read through the instructions with the children to ensure that they understand the task and its purpose.

This exercise follows on naturally from the two previous pages but introduces an emphasis on the importance of writing at an acceptable speed. The tasks set are designed to consolidate their work on self-assessment and correct writing but also to create an awareness of the need to write well at a speed that allows them to meet the many demands made upon them.

A number of children will be needed as timekeepers while others copy out the rhyme or the teacher may prefer to act as timer. A group of children might conduct the 'letters per minute' experiment at the same time as others perform this exercise. As a further development, children might explore the effects of practice and fatigue on their performance.

Pages 12–15

Writing and spelling: Magic or marker *e*

Now that the pupils are thoroughly familiar with the full Nelson joined handwriting style, the link between consistent handwriting habits and good spelling is introduced. Children of this age should already be familiar through their reading with the modifying effect that a final *e* has on a medial vowel when only one consonant separates them.

A page is devoted to *a*, *i*, *o* and *u* as medial vowels and, on each page, numerous examples of words containing the spelling rule are provided.

Teachers should read through the instructions on the page and discuss them with the children. The lists of words should be read through to establish correct pronunciation, and the opportunity should be taken to broaden children's vocabulary by discussing unfamiliar words with them. The children should then write out the lists of words carefully while making a conscious effort to develop both a visual and a motor memory of the spelling pattern on that page.

Pages 12, 13 and 14 each conclude with a short prose passage. These passages should be read through and discussed before the pupils are instructed to write out the passage carefully and well. Finally, the children should underline all the words in the passage that conform to the spelling rule on that page.

The words underlined should be as follows:

12 name race space date (4 words)
13 wife Mike drive arrive alive time wise advice (8 words)
14 strode slope strove code broke drove home note Rome (10 words)

Page 15

More self-assessment and writing at speed

An additional objective is pursued on this page. Following the exercise on spelling, a traditional weather rhyme is presented as a basis for further practice in self-assessment and in writing well at speed. The rhyme should be read through and discussed so that its implications are fully understood before the children proceed to perform the writing task.

Pages 16 and 17

Writing and spelling: words beginning *ch*, *sh*, *th* and *wh*; *ch*, *sh* and *th* within words (consonant digraphs)

Further attention is given to the link between writing and spelling through work on consonant digraphs. Although this technical term is not used in the pupils' book, teachers might like to introduce the term and to demonstrate the way in which the two letters together form a sound which cannot be achieved by blending the individual sounds of two consonants. It should be pointed out that on page 16 the consonants occur at the beginning of words while on page 17, they occur within words.

The lists of words should be read through to establish correct pronunciation, and the meanings of any words unfamiliar to the children should be explained to them. The children should then write out the lists bearing in mind the importance of trying to develop both a visual and a motor memory of the spelling patterns. To this end, teachers might want to introduce the strategy suggested by Margaret Peters in her *Diagnostic and Remedial Spelling Manual*. She recommends a four-step routine:

1. Looking carefully at a word and trying to memorise it
2. Covering the word

3. Writing the word from memory
4. Checking for accuracy

At the foot of both pages are three sentences, each with two words omitted. These sentences should be read through and the instructions discussed. The children should then write out each sentence including two words, selected from the lists above, to complete them.

The missing words are as follows:

page	
16	1. thief, shop (church, theatre) 2. whistle, chase 3. white, whale
17	1. father, pushchair 2. splash, bath 3. bishop, cloth

Page 18

Writing with purpose: A Christmas shopping list

Another aim of the revised *New Nelson Handwriting* is to demonstrate the many purposes for which writing is used. The writing of a shopping list is an activity with which most children are familiar, and a list of Christmas presents should certainly be of interest. The list should be read through and discussed before the children write it out in the conventional format.

Additional activities might include:

- Writing a list of twelve presents for one's self
- Writing a list of twelve presents for others
- Choosing a particular kind of shop and writing a list of items to buy from it
- Writing a list of groceries to be bought

Page 19

Writing with purpose: A recipe for banana whip

The recipe illustrates another function of writing. It should be read through and discussed with the children before they write it out carefully.

The exercise could end there but many teachers will want to arrange for their pupils, perhaps working in groups, to try out the recipe. Cooking and other food studies are becoming increasingly common in Junior schools where parents are able to give some time to come in and work with groups of children. In classes where this is possible the children could be encouraged to build up their own collection of recipes.

Pages 20–24

Writing and spelling (consonant blends)

Teachers should explain that sounds associated with consonant blends are achieved by blending together the individual sounds of the two consonants.

This is in contrast with consonant digraphs (see the notes to pages 16 and 17). The lists of words on each page should be read aloud to establish correct pronunciation and to emphasise the sound of the consonant blends. Unfamiliar words and the follow-up exercises should be discussed thoroughly. In this way the exercise should consolidate the spelling and vocabulary lesson as well as provide handwriting practice.

Page 20

Words beginning *bl*, *cl*, *fl*, *gl* and *pl*

Alphabetical order is revised in this exercise. Teachers should explain that, when the first two or more letters are the same, then the third, fourth or even fifth letters are considered.

The correct order of words in the exercises is as follows:

gl glade gleam glen glide glory glove
pl plain plan plenty plot plough
bl blade blanket bleed bless blitz block blouse blunder blunt

Page 21

Words beginning *br*, *cr*, *dr*, *gr* and *tr*

Children are encouraged to look carefully at the spelling of the words in these sentences. Words in the sentences that also appear in the lists and are to be underlined are as follows:

1. truck driver broken brakes crashed trunk
2. crew grumbled bread crumb

Page 22

Words beginning *sc*, *sk*, *sl*, *sm*, *sn*, *sp*, *st* and *sw*

Teachers should make sure that children understand what is meant by the definition of a word.

The two words which match the definitions are:

1. sledge 2. sculpture

Page 23

Words ending *ck*, *nd* and *ng*

Unlike the consonant blends on pages 20–22 which occurred at the beginning of words, the consonant blends on this page occur in the middle or at the end of words.

The words to match the three definitions are:

1. thunder 2. hand 3. clock

Page 24

Words containing *st*, *nk* and *nt*

On this page too the consonant blends come in the middle or at the end of words.

The words which match the three definitions are:

1. mint 2. history 3. monk

Page 25

Words containing double letters: *ff*, *ll* and *ss* (double consonants)

Teachers should point out that double consonants occur in the middle or at the end of words. The correct method of writing double *f* should be revised as it is a frequent source of difficulty. Teachers should emphasise that two '*s*'s together do not join. The lists of words and the sentences should then be read through and discussed with the children.

The words to match the three definitions are:

1. boss 2. cliff 3. holly

Page 26

Capital letters and proper nouns

The main function of this page is to provide revision and encourage improvement in the writing of capital letters. Practice is contrived through exercises which provide a check on spelling and encourage an interest in general knowledge.

The days of the week and the months of the year are words that children of this age might be expected to spell correctly. The list of countries presents an interesting challenge for the children who should be allowed to consult an atlas. Similarly, they may be permitted to use an atlas to help them make the list of towns and cities. These do not necessarily have to be restricted to places in any one country.

The last exercises should lead to children asking each other how they spell their names and this concern to get it right should be encouraged. Finally, having collected a list of names spelt correctly, the children should write them out again in alphabetical order. The work on this page also serves to emphasise that proper nouns must begin with capital letters.

Page 27

Self-assessment and speed writing: A calendar rhyme

This page provides another opportunity for pupils to assess the quality of their own writing and to endeavour to write more quickly without making careless mistakes. If letters and joins are formed correctly and rhythmically, quicker writing should still be legible and pleasant to look at even though it may not be as regular and precise as writing produced more painstakingly.

The calendar rhyme should be read through and discussed. It may usefully be committed to memory as the facts contained in it are often needed. The sentence beginning 'The quick brown fox' was selected for the speed exercise as it includes all 26 letters of the alphabet.

Page 28

Revision of spelling rules and joins

This exercise has been devised as a puzzle. The children must first decide which word is intended. Then they must decide which two letters have been omitted from each word and finally they must take care to make all joins correctly when they write out the words.

The page number relating to each line of examples is indicated so that children can check for themselves that they have chosen the right word, spelled it correctly and made the joins properly. Checking their work is part of the developing policy of self-assessment. Pupils should correct any mistakes by rewriting the incorrect word.

The correct words are as follows:

space became escape brave
tribe smile exercise quite
globe smoke stone *or* stove vote froze
cube include duke fuse
chain shady thank where
machine touch splash fisher *or* father
blanket clever flavour flight
bread crown grand driver
skeleton sleep special steady
wreck quick stand beyond
castle history thank donkey
cliff toffee yellow grass

Page 29

Revision of numerals: Lengths of rivers and sums

The main aim of this page is to provide revision of numerals so that teachers can check that all their pupils can make the numerals confidently, correctly and quickly. However, the two exercises included provide interesting and purposeful activities.

1. The approximate lengths of ten major rivers are given in random order. The children should order the ten rivers on rough paper and then write out a fair copy of the list in ascending order:

	miles
River Clyde	106
River Thames	210
River Seine	473
River Rhine	800
River Ganges	1500
River Murray	1600
River Volga	2325
River Mississippi	2350
River Nile	4145
River Amazon	4195

2. Three sums have been includes so that children can be reminded of the vital importance of forming figures clearly and setting them out neatly.

Answers: 1. 17,128 2. 379 3. 18,774

Page 30

Writing with purpose: Setting out a letter

It is expected that children will already have had occasion to write letters for various reasons. This exercise draws attention to the conventions of letter writing while the content of the letter is intended to stimulate pride in writing well.

It may be helpful if the teacher also demonstrates the conventional lay-out on the blackboard. The letter should be read through and both its content and the arrangement on the page discussed before the children write it out carefully.

Once an interest in letter writing has been stimulated through this exercise teachers might create opportunities for children to write letters to people who might reasonably be expected to reply. It is helpful to advise children to draft their letters and then to look over their work for errors of spelling, punctuation etc. before they copy out the corrected draft carefully.

Pages 31 and 32

Poetry and prose as models for revision

Pupils' Book 2 concludes with a poem, and a page of prose as models for final revision practice. The pieces have been selected with the chlidren's enjoyment in mind. They should be read aloud well before being discussed with the children. The children should then write them out with care and pride.

Conclusion

If the policy of encouraging self-assessment which runs through this scheme is successful, children will check over their work and pick out any faults. Some children may then wish to write the piece again and improve their performance. However, many children will need to be prompted by the teacher to be critical of their own standards and, finally, it will be for the teacher to judge whether a particular piece of work is acceptable for the particular child. It is important to remember that it is equally harmful to demand more than a child can give as it is to accept less than the best.

Pupils' Book 3

Contents

Pupils' Book 3 covers the following:

- Revision of correct posture and pencil grip
- Pattern making to revise good writing techniques
- Revision of lower-case alphabet, capital letters and numerals
- Revision of all joins and the break letters
- A reduction in the size of writing
- Introduction of a slight slope to the right
- Additional spelling practice
- More exercises in self-assessment
- Introduction of writing with pen and ink

List of contents

Further practice of these items will be found in the Junior Copymasters. Relevant copymasters for further practice are indicated in brackets. A full chart cross-referencing the Junior Copymasters to Pupils' Book 3 will be found on p. 142.

Using Pupils' Book 3

This book is intended to be used at third year Junior level i.e. with pupils aged 9–10 years. However, teachers may find that some children are ready to use Pupils' Book 3 at an earlier or later stage. It is therefore essential that teachers are familiar with the content and sequence of the whole scheme and that they have studied this manual. They will then be prepared to take individual pupils back to an earlier book if it is more appropriate to their level of attainment. It is assumed that pupils beginning Book 3 will be able to make all letters and joins correctly and at a reasonable speed.

Page by page guide

Pages 1–4

Revision

The first four pages are devoted to revision of such basic matters as posture, pencil grip and general writing habits followed by revision of letter formation, joins and the full Nelson handwriting style. These notes for teachers are deliberately brief but teachers can refer to the notes for teachers on pages 1–4 of Pupils' Book 2 for further advice. While the children are working through these pages, teachers should be evaluating standards of performance and assessing readiness to proceed to the next stage i.e. reducing the size of writing and introducing a slight slope. Those children revealing fundamental faults at this stage should receive intensive remedial help or, if necessary, be taken back to repeat earlier lessons.

Page 5

Sloping writing

The notes on the pupils' page explain to the children the next stage in their development as writers: a reduction in the size of their writing and the introduction of a slight slope (6°) to the right. A model of the Nelson style modified in this way is provided for study and discussion. It may be helpful for teachers to demonstrate and emphasise the difference between the previously upright writing and the sloped version on the blackboard.

The traditional poem 'Matthew, Mark, Luke and John' has been chosen for this purpose and it is assumed that it will be read through and discussed before the children start to write. The pupils should then practise writing the poem endeavouring to effect an acceptable degree of slope. After each attempt they should appraise their work carefully for correct formation of letters and joins as well as for size of writing and degree of slope.

Page 6

More sloping practice

Examples of patterns already familiar in their upright versions are now introduced with a slope of 6°. The children should be encouraged to practise these and other modified patterns to increase their confidence, speed and rhythm.

The poem 'Spring Song' is then provided as a further model for practising sloped writing. After reading and discussion it should be practised until an acceptable standard is achieved.

Page 7

Sloping letters and numerals

Now that the children have attained a reasonable proficiency in producing joined handwriting with a slight slope they are expected to make unjoined letters with a similar slope. Sloping lower-case and capital letters are provided for practice. Similarly, sloped versions of numerals are included and further practice in sloped writing is achieved through a check on the spelling of some important number words.

Pages 8–11

Sloping writing and checking spelling

On these four pages further practice in writing the sloped style is combined with spelling practice. Lists of words are provided which draw attention to common spelling patterns. The words should be read through to establish correct pronunciation and the sound/symbol correspondence of the vowel digraphs and vowel modifiers involved. The meanings of any unfamiliar words should be discussed with the children.

As pupils write out the lists of words they should be concerned to effect the right degree of slope and to make all letters and joins correctly. At the same time they should be encouraged to say each word silently to themselves as they write it and thus to internalise the sound/symbol relationships.

Page 8

Vowel digraphs: *ee*, *ea*, *oo*

Special attention should be drawn to the second set of *ea* words in which *ea* is pronounced differently.

The exercise for consolidation is a simple one. The sentence should be written out and all words containing *ee*, *ea* or *oo* should be underlined.

The number of words to be underlined is 7.

Page 9

Vowel digraphs: *oa*, *oi*, *oy*, *ou*, *ai* and *ay*

Special attention should be drawn to the second set of *ou* words in which *ou* is pronounced differently. Again the exercise consists of writing out the sentence and underlining the words containing digraphs studied on the page.

The number of words to be underlined is 5.

Page 10

Vowel digraphs: *ei* and *ie*; vowel modification: *as*, *ar* and *alm*

Consideration of the letter combination *as* may prompt an interesting discussion on regional dialects. The way in which letter *r* modifies vowels is introduced through the letters *ar* and special attention should be paid to the second set of *ar* words in which pronunciation contrasts with that of the first set.

The consolidation exercise on this page requires pupils to use specified words, drawn from the spelling lists, in sentences of their own construction. The children should be reminded to write carefully but should also be encouraged to make their sentences full and interesting. It will be for the teacher to judge whether or not each child works to capacity.

Page 11

Vowel modification: *al*, *all*, *air*, *are*, *ear*, *er*, *ir*, *or* and *ur*

The concept of vowel modification is further explored. Special attention should be paid to two very common words which do not conform to the general pronunciation: *shall* and *are*.

Page 12

The size of letters and direction of strokes

The purpose of this page is to continue the process of making pupils aware of the qualities of good handwriting and to reinforce the habit of self-assessment. Attention is therefore paid to uniformity in the size of letters, to proper proportions for ascenders and descenders and to the desirability of making down-strokes and up-strokes parallel.

A group of words and finally an old weather saying are models for practice. The weather saying should be read and discussed by the class together. The rhyme may at first seem contradictory so teachers should encourage further thought before explaining that normally in Britain the coldest weather in winter comes after the shortest day.

Page 13

Spacing of letters, words and lines

This page is designed to draw attention to another characteristic of good handwriting: spacing. The advice on the pupils' page explains the criteria for good spacing but teachers should emphasise that spacing must be uniform. The space between letters is determined by the width of a well-made basic join. The space between words in a sentence is generally recommended to be the space a lower-case *a* would occupy. The question of space between lines only arises when plain paper is used, a good reason for ensuring, at least, an occasional use of unlined paper for handwriting. When writing on plain paper lines should be twice as far apart as the height of letter *a*.

Exercises are provided for children to practise writing with correct spacing and to assess their own performance. The final model is another old weather saying which should be read and discussed before writing. Again pupils should assess their own work paying particular attention to spacing.

Page 14

A self-assessment exercise

This is the third consecutive page contributing to the habit of self-assessment. The prose passage is a model for the children to write. They are also provided with a check list against which to assess their performance.

The passage is taken from *My Family and Other Animals* by Gerald Durrell which is a charming and vivid account of the author's observations of, and adventures with animals. The extract should be read and discussed in the usual way and may well stimulate a desire to hear more of the book.

Page 15

Sloping writing at speed

As one of the declared aims of Nelson handwriting is to equip pupils with writing skills that will serve all their needs for study and life, the question of speed must be considered. On this page attention is focussed on the importance of writing at speed without sacrificing legibility.

The model for practice should prove interesting to the pupils when it is read and discussed before writing. As well as measuring writing speed, children should use the checklist on page 14 to assess the quality of their quicker writing. While it is inevitable that writing more speedily produced will be less uniform and precise than painstaking efforts, too great a disparity in standard is unacceptable and indicates the need for further practice.

Pages 16–20

Writing with ink

Children who have learned to hold and use a pencil in the correct manner and who have acquired satisfactory habits of posture and relaxation will have little difficulty in learning to use an ink pen. If a fountain pen with a smooth, firm nib is used, the very minimum of help from the teacher will be required. On no account should a finely pointed, flexible nib be used.

In this scheme, a pen with a firm nib which produces unshaded writing, is used as a means of introducing children to writing with ink. A variety of mono-line instruments is also likely to be used and these will be discussed in more detail later. The change to the use of a square-edged nib which produces a more satisfying and attractive style of writing is dealt with in Pupils' Book 4 but can be introduced earlier if desired.

Children should be given the following advice:

1. The pen must be held lightly.
2. It should press very lightly on the paper.
3. It should be held in the same way as a pencil.
4. It should make an angle of about 45° with the paper and the end should point along the line of the forearm to a point beyond the right shoulder.
5. It should not be turned or twisted by the fingers; the angle it makes with the paper should remain constant.

If the children are to transfer from pencil to pen and ink with confidence, these requirements should only be mentioned briefly before they start to use the pen. Detailed instruction and attention should be left until a start is made on the more formal pattern exercises on pages 16 and 17. The first step in learning to cope with ink is plentiful practice in undirected scribbling and pattern exercises to develop confidence and skill in using the pen. There are some important points for the teacher to consider:

1. Who is to supply the fountain pen?
   Many children are willing and able to supply their own but they and their parents will welcome advice about a suitable pen and nib.
2. The need for a reserve supply of pens in case a child forgets to bring a pen to school, a pen breaks or otherwise fails.
3. The need to establish 'safe' procedures for refilling pens. A supply of cartridges should be available, but, for those children using filler pens, a convenient place should be found in the room for a bottle of ink to be available.

Even the preliminary practice recommended should be done on good quality paper as inferior paper does not give satisfying results with ink. When sufficient informal practice has been carried out, the children should proceed to the more formal and directed pattern exercises on pages 16 and 17 of the Pupils' Book before proceeding to writing words in ink.

Although it is recommended that children be encouraged to use a fountain pen for much of this practice it is likely that a variety of writing instruments will be available to the children. Ballpoint pens, nylon-tipped pens, fibre-tipped pens, felt-tipped pens and roller ball pens are all generally available and in wide use. Therefore, unless a school has decided on the dubious policy of banning the use of all mono-line instruments, it will be necessary to encourage similar experimentation to develop mastery and control of whichever instrument is being used. The general principles of good handwriting will still apply but scribbling and pattern making exercises are especially useful in providing necessary experience in discovering appropriate angles and pressures for proper control of low-friction nibs such as these.

During the time spent experimenting with pen and ink and working through pages 16–20, children should continue using pencil for other work. When a satisfactory mastery of ink has been achieved they should be encouraged to use ink for much of their work.

Page 16

Sloping writing with ink

Children are reminded of the importance of good fundamental writing habits. They are provided with models of scribbling exercises and patterns to reproduce after they have had sufficient experience of free experimentation.

Page 17

Using the pen correctly

Further attention is given to good writing habits. The need for light, smooth movements is stressed. Several formal patterns and a sentence provide models for further practice.

Page 18

Writing well with ink

Lord Tennyson's poem 'The Eagle' is the model for writing practice on this page. The poem should be introduced through a good reading and be discussed with the children before they write it out. In addition to the criteria for correct writing listed on page 14, the children have now to consider the light and smooth handling of the pen necessary for writing well in ink. They are encouraged to evaluate their writing and to improve their performance by repeating the exercise.

Page 19

Time and Space

The list of words connected with time provides another opportunity to practise writing well with pen and ink. As usual the words should be read through and discussed with the children before they begin writing.

The children are then required to think of 20 words connected with space. It is suggested that children work in pairs. They should form the list on rough paper and then arrange the words into alphabetical order. After checking spelling in their dictionaries they should then write out the list carefully in columns. Finally the children could jointly assess their writing against the list of criteria for good handwriting on page 14.

Page 20

Writing with ink quickly and well

This page is designed to stimulate interest in writing quickly with pen and ink without sacrificing legibility. Children should be encouraged to time themselves each time they write out the limerick and also to assess the quality of their writing.

Pages 21–25

More spelling and writing practice

These pages are designed to provide further practice in using ink and, at the same time, to revise spelling patterns. On each page there are lists of words to be read through and discussed, both with regard to the meaning of the words included and the spelling rule featured. Each page concludes with an exercise to consolidate the lesson of the page.

Page 21

Triple consonant blends

The spelling rule practised on this page is the blending of triple consonants. The exercise consists of copying out each sentence but substituting a word from the lists for each word underlined. The pupils should be advised to modify the word they select by adding *s*, *ed* or *ing* etc. if necessary. The substitutions are:

1. scrambling scrub scratched
2. stray stream stroll

Page 22

Silent letters

On this page attention is drawn to silent letters so pupils should be encouraged to look closely at each word as it is read out and to decide which letter is not heard. The substitutions in the sentences are:

1. phantom physician
2. whoop whimper

Page 23

More spelling

Each line of spelling on this page draws attention to an unusual sound/ symbol relationship. Reading and discussion should increase the children's awareness of these relationships. In many classes the invitation to think of other words containing the same spelling pattern may best be met through group or class discussion with the teacher acting as judge.

Page 24

Rules for forming plurals by adding *s* or *es*

Children's mastery of these rules is tested by the task at the foot of the page. As well as checking the correctness of the plural forms, the quality of the writing should also be assessed. Correct plurals are:

banjos boys churches glasses heroes pianos
potatoes schools streets watches witches wizards

Page 25

More rules for forming plurals

Irregular plurals and words ending with *f* are listed as models for discussion and writing practice. The concluding exercise requires children to rewrite a sentence making all nouns plural. They should be advised to omit *a* and *an* and to leave numbers unspecified. The plural version of the sentence will then be as follows:

Dogs chased sheep across fields and through farmyards where oxen stood watching mice.

Page 26

A self-assessment exercise

This poem by Robert Graves is provided as a model for another self-assessment exercise. The poem should be read carefully to the class and discussed with them before writing practice begins. The children should be encouraged to observe a cabbage-white butterfly in flight if at all possible. After writing the children should assess their work in the light of the criteria listed on page 14 and practise to correct any fault observed.

Page 27

Writing with purpose: Nature observation

The leaves and fruit of two very common trees have been selected for observation so that the leaves and fruits will be familiar to most children and so that it should be possible to find photographs and drawings and even, in due season, actual specimens from these trees.

The description of the oak leaves and fruits should be read and discussed before children write it out carefully. The children should then study a photograph, drawing or, preferably, the specimens of the horse chestnut. They should then make a rough draft of their description along the lines of the one provided for the oak. This draft should be checked and any mistakes in grammar, spelling or punctuation corrected before it is written out carefully. Finally the children should check their writing against the list of criteria for good handwriting on page 14.

Pages 28–30

Prefixes and suffixes

These three pages of spelling and writing practice draw attention to the effect of adding prefixes and suffixes to words. The words and definitions listed should be read out together with the new word formed by the addition of the prefix or suffix. The meanings should be discussed, and then children should write out the modified form of each word.

Page 28

Prefixes that make opposites

When the sentences are written out the following words should be substituted:

1. dislike unkind
2. unconscious disorderly
3. impossible illegible

Page 29

Prefixes that indicate number

The children are required to write out each definition carefully and to write the word defined by it. They should be encouraged to use their dictionaries to check meaning and spelling. The words defined are as follows:

1. centimetre 2. bicycle 3. tripod 4. triangle 5. centurion
6. bi-annual 7. biped 8. centipede.. 9. tricycle

Page 30

Suffixes

On this page the rules for adding suffixes to verbs are considered. The examples should first be read through and discussed with the children. They should then write them out to internalise the spelling patterns and to practise writing well.

Page 31

Records as a model for practice

A list of records from the *Guinness Book of Records* is provided to give purposeful practice in writing numerals in ink. (It may be that some of these records have since been broken). It is also included as a source of interest and discussion. As a follow-up exercise children could find some more examples of records to write up carefully in their notebooks.

Page 32

Final models for practice

Pupils' Book 3 concludes with two short pieces that should stimulate thought and discussion as well as provide final models for practice of writing the sloped Nelson joined style in ink.

The children should be given the opportunity of writing these and other poems, paying considerable attention to all the qualities of good writing but writing as fluently as possible.

The arrangement of material on the page in an attractive and pleasing manner should always be encouraged.

Additional work

If there is sufficient time after the work detailed in this book has been covered, the teacher should revise and consolidate the work covered in this part of the scheme.

Assessments should again be made of the quality and fluency of the writing of each child. While remedial instruction is given to the less able, the better writers should be set exercises to develop the quality and fluency of their writing further. Aimless practice by the better pupils must be avoided.

All children should be encouraged to make patterns to decorate notices and pages of work. The children should continue to acquire the habit of self-assessment and teachers should make checks on their writing speeds at regular intervals as well as provide occasional incentives for the production of aesthetic, well-presented writing.

Pupils' Book 4

Contents

Pupils' Book 4 covers the following:

- Revision of posture and penhold
- Revision of problem letters
- More self-assessment exercises and speed tests
- Poetry and prose as models for practice
- Introduction of shaded writing
- An emphasis on careful presentation of written work
- Inclusion of several different set hands to encourage individuality of style.

List of contents

Further practice at the Pupils' Book 4 level will be found in Junior Copymasters 26–32. A full chart cross-referencing the Junior Copymasters to Pupils' Book 4 will be found on p. 142.

Using Pupils' Book 4

Pupils' Book 4 is the final book in the Nelson handwriting scheme and by the time pupils start to use this book they should have developed a sufficient degree of muscular co-ordination to enable them to write well with speed and rhythm. The main aim of this scheme is to help all children achieve this basic standard. Throughout the Pupils' Books, there has been a strong emphasis upon correct letter formation, fluent well-formed joins, uniformity of size, slope and spacing and the importance of legibility at reasonable speed.

In Pupils' Book 4, after some necessary revision, the children are introduced to shaded writing and examples of aesthetically pleasing set hands. They are encouraged to experiment and develop a style of their own, which may perhaps be based on one of the examples, to use on more formal occasions. However, they should be advised to continue practising the legible, fast-flowing, rhythmic and individual basic style which they have gradually developed through the course. It is this basic style which will enable them to cope with most of the varied writing demands that will arise in school and in adult life.

Although children are likely to continue using pencil for some of their work it is expected that they will use ink for the exercises in this book. Pupils and their parents may need advice about suitable pens and nibs, especially for the straight-edged or broad nib work. It will also be necessary for the teacher to organise reserve supplies of pens and nibs against the event of a forgotten or broken pen. A supply of cartridge refills and a system for safely filling fountain pens will also prove valuable.

Page by page guide

Pages 1 and 2

Revision of posture, penhold and patterns

Children will benefit from a considerable amount of informal practice to enable them to gain confidence and control over the pen. The angle of the pen to paper should receive special attention as it is crucial to successful writing with pen and ink.

Pages 3–6

Revision of letters, numerals, joins and the size and slope of letters

On these four pages children are shown how to appraise their own writing and advised on acceptable standards of performance in the following important aspects of handwriting:

a) The relative size of letters

b) The slope of writing

c) Correct formation of all letters and numerals

d) Correct making of all joins

e) Legible writing at speed

By this stage, children should be able to read and follow the instructions on each page independently. The teacher's role, therefore, is to supervise practice, to encourage self-appraisal, including a decision to repeat an exercise if necessary, to intervene and demonstrate as necessary and to refer pupils with fundamental faults back to relevant exercises in earlier books.

The weather sayings on page 6 should be read and discussed before it is used for writing practice to revise all aspects of handwriting.

Pages 7–10

Revision of problem letters

Page 7

Oval letters: *a*, *c*, *d*, *g*, *o* and *q*

The correct formation of the anticlockwise oval shape which is the basis of these six letters is the subject of this page. After illustration and practice of the basic shape, letters and words containing this oval shape are then provided as models for further practice.

The page concludes with a short rhyme, 'The Difference' which should be read aloud and discussed before serving as a model for careful practice.

Page 8

The letters *p* and *b*

A clockwise oval forms part of the letters *b* and *p*. After illustration and practice of the basic oval shape, letters and words containing *b* and *p* are provided for further practice.

The page concludes with a joke. It has been included to give variety and amusement.

Page 9

The letters *s* and *e*

Minor amendments to *s* and *e* are examined. Words containing these variations are provided for writing practice.

Page 10

The letters *r*, *f*, *j*, *k* and *y*

Because these letters sometimes give rise to problems they are afforded special attention here.

The Post Office slogan at the foot of the page dates from the early days of the postal service in the U.S.A. when the mail was despatched on foot, on horseback or by coach. The Post Office couriers prided themselves on their determination to deliver the mail even in the face of East Coast blizzards. The slogan should be read and discussed before being written out carefully.

There are 4 '*f*'s and 10 '*r*'s in this piece.

Page 11

A self-assessment exercise

The first ten pages of Pupils' Book 4 have been devoted to revision of all aspects of the Nelson joined style and practice in the use of pen and ink. This page is designed to develop the practice of self-assessment further.

First the children are required to copy a description of the correct position of the arm and hand when writing. They are then asked to examine their writing and check it carefully under the four main headings of letters, joins, words and lines. They should be encouraged to repeat the exercise if they are not satisfied with any aspect of their writing. The role of the teacher is to supervise the process and intervene with praise or criticism as necessary.

The process of writing and self-appraisal is then repeated using the limerick as a basis for practice. It is, of course, assumed that both examples will be read through and discussed before handwriting practice begins.

Page 12

Writing quickly: A speed test

Children are encouraged to compare and contrast painstaking writing with writing at speed. They are first asked to write a sentence very carefully and then write it again very quickly. In comparing the two sentences they should be made to feel that while the writing produced at speed may not be as precise and uniform, provided that it is legible and properly formed, it is perfectly acceptable. The concept of a dual standard, a conscious best hand and a quick, functional hand, is an important one to establish. However, careless scribble is not acceptable at any time.

The short prose extract by C. S. Lewis is provided as an example of a calligrapher's quick hand and is intended to be examined and discussed to support the points made in the paragraph above. The significance of the statement should also be discussed with the children.

Finally there is a letter-count speed test based on the first line from the nursery rhyme, 'Mary had a little lamb'. Again, legibility and reasonably accurate letter formation are to be emphasised at the same time as the importance of increasing speed.

Pages 13–18

Prose and poetry as models for sustained writing practice in the Nelson joined style using pen and ink

In each case the piece should first be read through and discussed with the children before writing practice begins. After they have finished writing it out the children should be encouraged to look over their work as in the other self-appraisal exercises on previous pages. If children are dissatisfied with their writing on any occasion they should be allowed to do it again and attempt to improve their work.

Page 13

'Tremendous Trifles'

This traditional poem should be read rhythmically and can be used for choral speaking in a number of ways. Then, in discussion, the idea of chain reaction would be explored, and children asked to think of other examples of interdependence in their experience.

Page 14

'He Who Knows'

This traditional poem from Persia should first be read and discussed at some length to ensure that it is understood before writing practice begins.

Page 15

Writing and science

Throughout Pupils' Books 1–4 ways have been sought to demonstrate some of the various uses of writing. In this example writing was used to record scientific observations.

The passage should be read through and discussed with the children before writing practice begins. The children might be interested to know more about the life and work of Charles Darwin.

As a follow-up exercise pupils might write up a piece of their own scientific observation in a 'set' hand for display.

Pages 16 and 17

'Numbers'

This double-page spread is devoted to a poem by Eleanor Farjeon. As usual, it should be read and discussed before the children use it as a model for sustained writing practice.

There are several points of interest in this poem that can be highlighted. For example, teachers might like to initiate discussion about the rhyming pattern, pointing out how the last line in the first three verses is the same while the last line of verse four rounds off the whole poem. They might also like to consider the way in which each verse has its own theme: stars, water, insects and numbers respectively. Finally, the way in which the concept of infinity is approached from hundreds to thousands and then from millions to no end of numbers might also be explored.

It will also be necessary to ensure that the pupils know what the 'Tail of the Bear' and 'The Waterman's Hat' are. The references to the 'Mexican Gulf' and the 'Lincolnshire Flat' will provide an opportunity to remind children of how to use an atlas, while the third verse may be used to start a discussion of the characteristics of an insect.

When the children have copied out this poem in their best 'set' hand, an activity which will require considerable care and sustained concentration, they should evaluate their writing against the usual criteria.

Page 18

Writing and mathematics

Writing for the purposes of recording and explaining mathematical thinking is explored on this page. An imaginary discussion about the difference between 10 feet and 3 metres on a motorway notice is the subject of the exercise. Many children will have noticed similar signs when driving along the motorways with their parents, and interesting discussion should accompany the reading of this page. Attention should be drawn to the formal setting out of the calculations involved in the comparison, and the importance of writing figures very clearly.

When the children have written the piece out in their best 'set' hand they should carry out the usual assessment procedure paying extra attention to the figures. A useful follow-up exercise would be to ask each child to think of a situation in their experience which required calculations to be done. They could then draft out an account of the situation together with the calculations involved. After the correction of any errors in spelling, grammar or punctuation, their accounts could be written out in best writing for a class display.

Pages 19–24

Shaded writing

These five pages introduce the use of the straight-edged or broad nib and provide practice in 'shaded' writing. Children whose achievement with pen and ink is only barely satisfactory may prefer to continue practising the basic style, but some children may be motivated by the introduction of a new element and the challenge and satisfaction of mastering the broad nib. The decision as to whether individuals should or should not undertake to write with a broad nib must be one for the child and teacher concerned to consider together. However, on no account should the development of a free cursive hand using an ordinary nib be neglected in favour of the formal calligraphic hand made with a broad-nibbed pen.

The teacher should emphasise that:

a) The square edge must always be flat on the surface of the paper.

b) The pen must always point in the same direction.

c) There is no change in pressure on the pen for up and down strokes.

At first the exercises on these pages should be written slowly and carefully. Children will benefit if the teacher is able to demonstrate the techniques involved by using lettering chalk on the blackboard.

Children will need a good deal of practice to master the art of writing with a broad nib and should be encouraged to experiment and practise until they feel comfortable and confident in using it. However, throughout this free practice, children should conform to the three basic points listed above. If the children are introduced to broad nib writing at the right time in their development in a school where aesthetic presentation and standards are highly regarded many children will become very enthusiastic and keen to master the art.

Some consideration will have to be given to the provision of the necessary nib. A fountain pen with interchangeable nib units is ideal and several companies market sets at reasonable prices. The author's experience has been that many children are both willing and able to provide their own instrument but the school will need a policy for catering for those pupils who cannot afford to purchase their own. Broad nibs are, of course, available for dip pens but, unless the nib is a reservoir type it can be frustrating to have to be continually dipping the pen in the ink.

Page 19

Shaded writing 1

Shaded writing is introduced through the comparison of a sentence written with an ordinary firm nib and the same sentence written with a broad nib. Discussion and observation supplemented by blackboard demonstration should establish that, when the nib is kept flat on the paper and at an angle of 45°, uphill strokes will be thin, downhill strokes will be thick and vertical strokes will be of medium thickness. This is illustrated in the Pupils' Book together with examples of the three thicknesses of line.

Some curved letters are illustrated next to show how, providing the three basic rules are adhered to, parts of a curved letter will display each of the three thicknesses. This aspect of shaded writing should also be demonstrated by the teacher.

The page concludes with some very simple stroke-making exercises for repeated practice to consolidate the good habits taught and to develop confidence and fluency with the broad nib.

Page 20

Shaded writing 2

This page continues with the teaching on page 19 and introduces the use of various widths of broad nib. Children should be encouraged to practice with fine, medium and broad nibs and to think about an appropriate width of nib for the size of their writing.

A sentence and some words are provided as models for the children to practice and they should be encouraged to repeat the exercises until they are satisfied with their achievement using all three grades of broad nib.

Pages 21–23

Shaded writing 3–5

Through these three pages broad nib models of all lower-case letters are provided arranged according to method of writing. The children are instructed to practise making them carefully. The pages conclude with words or a sentence to be practised repeatedly until they can be made with a smooth, quick and fluent movement.

Page 24

Shaded writing: Capitals

Plain capitals remain the same as they have been throughout the scheme except that, when formed with a broad nib correctly used, the different parts of each letter will be of varying thickness.

Pupils should not experience any difficulty in writing shaded capitals provided the three basic rules are kept:

a) The square edge must always be flat on the surface of the paper.

b) The pen must always point in the same direction.

c) There should be no change of pressure on the pen for up and down strokes.

The children are instructed to practise making basic strokes. They are then given models of all capital letters and figures from which to practise. The page concludes with a sentence written in shaded capitals as a model for practice and as a reminder of the circumstances in which capital letters are used.

Page 25

A self-assessment exercise and speed test

Although the models for practice are written with a broad nib, the practice work and speed tests can also be done by children using an ordinary nib if they have not progressed to the broad nib. Indeed, other children may want to attempt this exercise more than once, using an ordinary nib, as well as the broad nib, to keep up their proficiency with the basic tool.

The first sentence is intended to remind children, and teachers, that unless practice in handwriting is undertaken with a conscious effort to improve standards it can be a waste of time and may even result in a deterioration in standards.

The speed test involves the now familiar weather saying, 'When the days begin to lengthen, Then the cold begins to strengthen'. Children should be reminded during discussion that for most English winters the saying is true although it seems, on first consideration, to be contradictory.

The page concludes with a simple scientific explanation of a rainbow. When this has been read and discussed it should be written as well as possible without painstaking slowness. The children should then go through their self-assessment procedure.

A useful follow-up exercise would be to invite the children to think of another natural phenomenon they have observed and understood. They could draft a brief explanation of it and then, after correction, write it up as well as they can for display.

Examples of possible subjects might include clouds, condensation, rivers, and the saltiness of the sea.

Page 26

Decorated capitals

Children who have enjoyed using the broad nib and have appreciated the increased aesthetic quality thus achieved will undoubtedly be enthusiastic to experiment with decorated capital letters. Since the final aim of the Nelson scheme is to encourage an individual style based on good principles, this is a good stage to encourage individuality and introduce children to a range of styles of decorated capitals and to encourage practice and experiment.

Three different styles of decorated capitals are illustrated on this page. They should be discussed and the teacher could profitably demonstrate some of them on the blackboard. The children should then practise some or all of the styles illustrated before deciding which they feel most confident in writing and which is most pleasing to them.

Finally they are invited to write out a list of the names of some famous buildings in the decorated style of their choice.

The public library will undoubtedly supply books containing further examples of other ornate styles of capital letters which may stimulate further experiment for those children who become interested in this kind of calligraphy.

It may be necessary to remind children that they need to continue to practise and use the plain Nelson capitals for everyday writing activities. They will have great difficulty in keeping pace with the writing demands made on them if they totally abandon the quick and easily made capitals of the Nelson style.

Page 27

Margins and spacing

The emphasis on this page is entirely on presentation and the arrangement of material on the page although, of course, the quality of the handwriting continues to be important. The children should already be aware of the effect of margins on the appearance of a page but here their attention is drawn to the need for forethought about side margins. In the example provided the initial letter of each line is arranged in a straight vertical line but, inevitably, the lines are of different lengths and the margin on the right side of the writing varies in width. However, the margin width at the longest line should be the same as the left-hand margin.

It is customary for the margin at the foot of the page to be wider than the one at the top but the relative proportions are a matter of personal preference. The children may enjoy decorating the margins with patterns or illustrations.

Pages 28–32

Examples of individual set hands

The last five pages of Pupils' Book 4 are devoted to examples of individual styles of handwriting. It is not intended that children be encouraged to try to copy all of the styles in turn but rather that they should first study all of the examples and then decide which, if any, they would prefer to influence their own development. It may be that some children who have become interested and successful in their attempts at broad nib calligraphy may feel encouraged by these examples to develop a style of their own. The real purpose of these final pages of the scheme is to promote interest in, and experimentation towards, the development of an individual style based on good fundamental principles.

In addition to studying and discussing the handwriting of these five pages there are other aspects of each page that should provide opportunities for useful work. Each page should be read through and discussed with the children. Various follow-up activities are suggested below.

Page 28

Ten-year-old Emma's account of her involvement in clubs and her other extra-curricular activities is a good starting point for discussion of the leisure time activities of the class. Children could then draft an account of their own favourite pursuits which, after correction, could be written out in a best 'set' hand for a display of calligraphy on this theme.

Pages 29, 31 and 32 (page 30 see below)

These three interesting accounts of hobbies may even stimulate enough interest to encourage some children to take them up. They also form a good starting point for discussion of hobbies in general and, once again, the children could write accounts of their own favourite hobbies. A classroom display of writing and objects connected with hobbies could then be mounted.

Page 30

This stimulating account of the variety of foods now available in multi-cultural Britain and the experience of eating out in restaurants of various nationalities should lead to lively discussion about likes and dislikes. A project in which children write about their preferences and collect and write out favourite menus and recipes might also prove successful. Such a project will be enhanced by allowing small groups to prepare some of the dishes mentioned. Fortunately, food studies are becoming much more common in Junior schools, often through the voluntary assistance of parents who come in and cook with small groups of children.

The Copymasters

Function of the Copymasters

Although the six Pupils' Books of *New Nelson Handwriting* are designed as a complete and comprehensive course, many teachers will find the supplementary material in the two books of copymasters a valuable source of additional practice and reinforcement. One obvious advantage of worksheets is their facility for allowing practice to be done on or alongside models of *Nelson Handwriting*. They allow easy repetition of a task with which a child is experiencing difficulty. They also provide an inexpensive opportunity to give *Nelson Handwriting* material for practice at home without fear of losing a Pupil's Book.

It will be necessary for teachers to give thought to the development of a convenient storage system for duplicated worksheets so that they are easily and readily available. It is also important to ensure that each child stores completed worksheets, perhaps in a cardboard folder. If no system is devised these sheets soon become crumpled or lost and pupils may get the impression that the work is not important. A suitable folder which can be decorated with handwriting patterns and in which the child's handwriting notebook is also stored will give a sense of purpose and motivation to this work.

The worksheets are designed to give additional practice at critical moments of development in the handwriting course. Detailed notes on their use will be found on the first side of each sheet but cross-reference to the Pupils' Books will also be found in this manual beside the contents list for each book.

Contents of the Copymasters

The charts on the following pages detail the contents of the two sets of copymasters and indicate the appropriate places for their use. The indications for their places of use are only approximate. It may often be found useful to return to a particular sheet at a later stage if a child is having problems and needs remedial help.

Infant Copymasters

Worksheets	Contents	Appropriate point of use and purpose
Sheets 1–15	**Pre-handwriting exercises**	Before and with Books A and B
1	Horizontal and vertical strokes	Structured practice in the essential pre-handwriting movement skills. The exercises can be used as part of the pre-handwriting programme before commencing Pupils' Book A (see page 62 of this manual). They also provide practice at the many patterns provided throughout Books A and B and can be used alongside these books. Children with fundamental movement problems should be referred back to these sheets throughout the infant stage of the course.
2	Horizontal and vertical strokes	
3	Zigzags	
4	Diagonals	
5	Anticlockwise circles	
6	Clockwise circles	
7	Anticlockwise loops	
8	Clockwise loops	
9	Clockwise and anticlockwise loops	
10	Swings and bridges patterns	
11	Revision of verticals, horizontals, swings and spirals	
12	Revision of bridges, zigzags, swings, horizontals	
13	*C* patterns	
14	*S* bends and curly tails	
15	Diagonals for *k*	
Sheets 16–23	**Lower-case letters and numerals**	With Book A
16	a c d g o q	Reinforcement practice for Book A of all lower-case letters in groups and the patterns from which they are derived as well as numerals. Children still having difficulty with correct letter formation at Book B stage should be referred back to these sheets.
17	e s f j u	
18	i k l t	
19	b p	
20	m n h r	
21	v w x y z	
22	1 2 3 4 5	
23	6 7 8 9 10	
Sheets 24–25	**Capital letters**	With Book B, pages 8–12
24	Capitals: A–P	Further practice at capitals taught in Book B, pages 8–12
25	Capitals: Q–Z and further practice	
Sheets 26–31	**Words and sentences**	With Book B, page 12 onwards Extra practice at writing words in sentences for use alongside Book B *after* capital letters have been taught.
Sheet 32	**Triple lines**	Whenever children need help in managing ascenders and descenders.

Junior Copymasters

Worksheets	Contents	Appropriate point of use and purpose
Sheets 1 and 2	**Assessment sheets**	Assessment sheets for monitoring individual pupil progress over the whole scheme
Sheets 3–6 3 4 5 6	**Pattern practice** Practice patterns 1 Practice patterns 2 Fun with pattern 1 Fun with pattern 2	Throughout Books 1–4 More complex patterns to provide practice and to develop fluency and control at all stages of Books 1–4
Sheet 7	**Infant Writing alphabet**	Start of Book 1 Reinforcement of Infant Writing alphabet as in Book 1 page 2 before commencing joined writing in Book 1.
Sheet 8	**Alphabet used in joint writing**	With Book 1 page 5 Further practice of Book 1 page 5
Sheets 9–17 9 10 11 12 13 14 15 16 17	**Practice of all joins** The basic join 1 The basic join 2 The second join The third join The fourth join The break letters Joins to *e* Joins to *s* Joins to and from *f*	After teaching joins in Book 1 Reinforcement of all the joining rules, as taught in Book 1. Revision at any time while using Books 1–4.
Sheets 18–22 18 19 20 21 22	**Sustained practice at upright joined writing** Checking on letter formation Checking on letter size Checking on spacing Checking on joins Checking on the angle of strokes	With Book 1 pages 31 and 32 and Book 2 Provides further sustained writing practice using all the rules and joins and develops an awareness of the criteria for assessing writing taught in Book 2. Practises upright writing.
Sheets 23–26 23 24 25 26	**Joined writing with a forward slope** Writing with a forward slope How well can you write? Writing quickly with pen and ink Individuality of style. Different writing tools	After teaching forward slope (Book 3 page 5) Extra practice at Book 3 level of joined writing with a forward slope. Practice at pen and ink writing taught from Book 3 page 16 onwards. Developing an individual style as in Book 4. Practice in using a range of different writing implements.
Sheets 27–32 27 28 Sheets 29–32	**Broad nib writing** Using the broad nib Presentation and shaded writing Presentation and decoration	With Book 4 page 19 on Further practice in broad nib writing as covered in Book 4 page 19 onwards With Book 4 Extra practice at laying out a letter, poetry and prose.

Glossary of terms

Anticlockwise: Moving in a curve from right to left.

Appraisal: To observe children's writing with a view to determining the effectiveness of the teaching policy.

Ascender: The part of a letter which extends above the height of the other 'ordinary' or 'x' height letters. The letters with ascenders are *b*, *d*, *f*, *h*, *k*, *l* and *t*.

Ball and stick: The highly undesirable practice of making letters like *a* and *d* in two separate parts, described respectively as ball and stick.

Basic join: The curved rising diagonal (45°) ligature which is the most common join in the *New Nelson Handwriting* style. See page 44.

Break letters: Those nine letters after which a join is not made, *b*, *g*, *j*, *p*, *q*, *s*, *x*, *y* and *z* in the *New Nelson Handwriting* style.

Bridges pattern: A rhythmically produced sequence of arches from left to right.

Broad nib: A nib with a straight edge which gives rise to variations in the width of pen strokes, also called a 'straight edged nib'.

Calligraphy: Handwriting as a fine art.

Capital letters: The forms of letters used at the beginning of sentences and proper nouns. They are never joined to lower-case letters in *New Nelson Handwriting*.

Clockwise: Moving in a curve from left to right.

Consonant blends: When two or three consonants occur together and the sound associated with the cluster is achievable by blending the individual consonant sounds together i.e. *br*at, *scr*unch.

'c' Pattern: The pattern made rhythmically by forming a continuous line of letter *c*'s.

Cross-laterality: Most people have dominant right hands and right eyes. Cross-laterality i.e. right hand/left eye or left hand/right eye dominance can lead to confusion over orientation of letters and over letter order in words.

Cursive: A running hand in which the letters are formed rapidly with a minimum of pen lifts.

Descender: The part of a letter which descends below the base line of the writing. The letters with descenders are *g*, *j*, *p*, *q* and *y*.

Diagonal pattern: The pattern rhythmically formed by joining left/right and right/left diagonal lines continuously across the page from left to right.

Digraph: When two letters occur together and the sound associated with the pair is not achievable by blending together the individual sounds of the letters i.e. *ch*at, r*ei*n.

Drafts: The practice of writing out ideas in a preliminary rough version for correction and editing before re-writing.

Fine motor skills: The muscular skills which enable a person to perform controlled and precise movements.

Gross motor skills: The muscular skills which enable a person to perform larger and less co-ordinated movements.

Hand-dominance: A natural tendency to use one hand, rather than the other hand, for fine motor activities.

Hooks: The small curved line that may be added to some lower-case letters where there is a natural tendency to join on to the next letter.

Inversion: The turning upside down of a letter so that it is mistaken for another e.g. writing *b*ie for *p*ie.

Joined writing: Writing which is cursive in that most of the lower-case letters are joined one to another.

Ligature: A stroke used to join two letters together. In well-formed handwriting all diagonal ligatures are parallel.

Lower-case: The form of letters of the alphabet which are not capital letters. These are sometimes called 'small' but this term is illogical.

Mirror-writing: Mirror-writing is writing which must be viewed in a mirror in order to be read. It most often occurs when left-handed writers commence writing on the right hand side of the page instead of on the left.

Mnemonics: A memory aid. Often a picture or a story to help a child remember the important facts about the sound/symbol relationship of letters.

Ordinary: In this sense it simply means lower-case letters which have neither ascenders nor descenders. Ordinary letters are 'x' height letters like *a*.

Parallel (of writing strokes)**:** Running in the same direction and always at the same distance apart.

Policy: A handwriting policy is a written statement of aims, objectives and methods. It is likely to be most effective when it reflects a concensus reached by all those who will be operating the policy.

Print script: Handwriting in which the unjoined lower-case letters correspond closely to the print used in children's reading books. Most print script letters are formed in one continous movement. Print script must, on no account be confused with 'ball and stick' which is to be strongly deprecated.

Programme: A detailed set of procedures or materials designed to help the achievement of a policy. A published scheme can form a programme.

Readiness: The point in the development of a child where a formal programme of instruction is likely to be fruitful.

Remedial: Special attention by a teacher to help a child overcome faults in writing techniques.

Rhythm: Regular and smooth movement characterised by strong and less strong elements with a definite absence of jerkiness.

Self-appraisal: Observation of children's writing and writing habits by the children themselves to determine the quality of their learning and the possible need for further practice.

Shaded writing: The name sometimes given to writing performed with a broad or straight-edged nib. Shaded writing is characterised by 'thicks' and 'thins'.

Speed of writing: An awareness of the need to write at speed enabling the writer to cope with the demands of school and life without sacrificing legibility and pleasant appearance.

Straight-edged nib: Another name for the broad nib used to give variations in the width of pen strokes.

Swash capitals: Highly decorated capital letters adorned with flourished strokes.

Swings pattern: The pattern formed rhythmically by making a continuous line of loops from left to right.

Tension: A strained tight feeling resulting perhaps from fear or insecurity and often revealed in over-tight pencil grip and cramped writing.

Tripod grip: The relaxed and correct way of supporting a writing implement between the thumb and next two fingers.

Uniformity: In writing – keeping all 'ordinary' letters the same height and width and keeping spaces between letters and words regular.

Visual perception: The ability to recognise and differentiate shapes. A factor to be borne in mind when assessing readiness for writing.

Vowel modifiers: A letter which, when occurring alongside a vowel or vowel digraph, modifies the vowel sound i.e. ha*l*t, a*r*ch.

'x' height: A technical term in the printing and publishing trades. The height of letters which have neither ascenders nor descenders: *a* is an 'x' height letter.

Bibliography

Ainscow, M. and Tweddle, D. (1979), *Preventing Classroom Failure* (John Wiley and Sons)

Bullock, Sir A. *et al.* (1975), *A Language for Life* (H.M.S.O)

Clark, M. M. (1959), *Teaching Left-handed Children* (University of London Press)

Durrell, G. (1959), *My Family and Other Animals* (Penguin Books)

Fagg, R. (1963), *Everyday Writing* (University of London Press)

Graves, Donald H. (1983), *Writing: Teachers and Children at Work* (Heinemann Educational Books)

Hall, N. (1987), *The Emergence of Literacy* (Hodder & Stoughton)

Kingman, Sir John *et al* (1988), *Report of the Committee of Inquiry into the Teaching of English Language* (H.M.S.O.)

Peters, M. (1975), *Diagnostic and Remedial Spelling Manual* (Macmillan)

S.C.D.C. (1989) *The National Writing Project* published materials (Nelson)

Smith, P. E. (1977), *Developing Handwriting* (Macmillan)

Wendon, L. (1984; first published 1973), *Pictograms* (Pictogram Supplies, Barton, Cambridge, CB3 7AY)

Index